50 Greatest Goalscorers

In the History of British Football

50 Greatest Goalscorers

Neil Beacom

 As far as possible all information is correct and up to date as at 19th September 2021. With apologies for any errors or omissions.

ISBN: 978-1-7398065-0-7

Published by Big VMac in conjunction with Writersworld. This book is produced entirely in the UK, is available to order from most book shops in the United Kingdom and is globally available via UK-based Internet book retailers and www.amazon.com.

Copy edited by Ian Large

Cover design by Jag Lall (www.jaglallart.com)

Grass photo credit: Michael Schwarzenberger from Pixabay
Ball photo credit: Michal Jarmoluk from Pixabay

Photographic and sketch credits:

Alamy Images
Belfast Telegraph Archives
Jag Lall
Sophia

www.writersworld.co.uk

WRITERSWORLD

2 Bear Close Flats
Bear Close
Woodstock
Oxfordshire
OX20 1JX
United Kingdom

☎ 01993 812500
☎ +44 1993 812500

The text pages of this book are produced via an independent certification process that ensures the trees from which the paper is produced come from well managed sources that exclude the risk of using illegally logged timber while leaving options to use post-consumer recycled paper as well.

Goals Folklore

Goalscoring has always been about the ball hitting the back of the net. However, in the beginning... there was no net. There was barely a goal. With no restrictions on height, first string was attached, replaced by tape, then from 1875 a crossbar was added between the posts.

An Evertonian engineer from Liverpool, John Alexander Brodie, changed everything. A year after his patent for goal netting had been granted and having already been used by the Football Association, the Football League introduced netting to goal structures in September 1891.

It is extraordinary to consider that, as the original 12 club division had been founded in 1888, three seasons of league football were completed without nets in goals.

During this time there had been many disputes over the legality of goals scored and goal netting was a much-welcomed innovation. The first top scorer was John Goodall with 21 league goals as Preston North End won the League and FA Cup double in the first season of English league football.

Since the origins of the Football Association there have been several changes of laws in the rules of the game that have both helped and hindered goal scoring, such as goalkeeper protection (not being able to bundle goalkeepers into the goal), alterations in the offside law, tackling from behind, the back pass rule, goal-line technology and, most recently, the introduction of Video Assistant Referee (VAR).

One thing has remained constant in all this time: The measurements of the width of the actual goal itself. Before netting and the crossbar there were just two upright posts and clear space all around. From 1863, the distance between each goal post has been unchanged, eight yards (24 feet) or 7.3152 metres. As every goalscorer knows, the goal does not move, it is always in the same place.

As a young boy I always had a fascination with goalscoring, particularly goalscorers. I would collect Panini stickers and football cards (at ten pence a packet with gum), comparing individual playing records, making my own football cards of favourites I was unable to find or swap and play fantasy football games with a Subbuteo ball. Inspired by the comic book goalscoring exploits of Roy Race in *Roy of the Rovers*, Hotshot Hamish in *Tiger* and Jon Stark, match winner for hire, in *Scoop*.

I would create my own imaginary goalscoring goalscorers.

Although my three comic book heroes are not included in our greatest goalscorers, I had to determine who would be and how to decide/establish which players to be featured. First of all, I considered the definition of a goalscorer. Over the history of British football there have been many goalscoring wingers and attacking midfielders (some of whom have actually found the onion bag more often than out and out forwards) but I decided not to include these players. Their responsibility was not solely to score goals as their abilities enabled them to create, and all goalscorers need a reliable and frequent supply line. As such, without these creative players there would certainly be less goals around.

So I excluded wide men exponents such as: Billy Meredith – 'The Prince of Wingers'; Cliff Bastin – legendary Arsenal star from the 1930s; Tom Finney – a one club man with 187 league goals for Preston North End and 30 more for England; Billy Liddell – one of only two players, the other being Stanley Matthews, to be part of both Great Britain sides in 1947 and 1955; George Best – the most talented footballer to emerge from the British Isles; Alan Woodward – goalscoring winger for Sheffield United; Peter Lorimer of Leeds United, with one of the hardest shots in football; and 'I wanna be' John Barnes, with over 150 career goals.

Likewise with attacking midfielders, footballers of the calibre of Bobby Charlton – one time record scorer for both Manchester United and England; Johnny Haynes of Fulham FC – the first £100 a week footballer; Martin Peters '10 years ahead of his time' – World Cup final scorer; Colin Bell, adored at Manchester City; inspirational Captain Marvel Bryan Robson; and John Wark, who had a knack of arriving at just the right time in the penalty area for Ipswich Town and Liverpool and shared a talking scene with Michael Caine in the film *Escape to Victory*.

More recently in the Premier League era we have been entertained by Southampton's Matthew Le Tissier who converted a record 47 out of 48 spot kicks and regularly held his own Goal of the Season competition, alongside 21st century box-to-box footballers Frank Lampard and Steven Gerrard.

Also, in the history of British football converted strikers to midfielders: Ray Kennedy and Paul Scholes, who continued to score in a deeper role and created even more goals for grateful teammates.

Upon making the decision of who did not qualify as a goalscorer, I had to decide/establish who would be considered for the 50 greatest. If this was to be based purely upon the 50 most prolific goalscorers in the history of British football, there would undoubtedly be more players from the 1920s and 1930s included. This was indeed the golden age of goalscoring. The inter-war years of 20 seasons of league football from 1919/20 to 1938/39 produced a goal average of 38.45 for the top-flight leading scorer. With defences adjusting to the new advantageous offside law, which was certainly beneficial for attacking players, to this day many clubs' individual and team goalscoring records still stand from this time.

Club record holders include, for most goals in a game Albert Whitehurst, 7 for Bradford City in March 1929; Robert 'Bunny' Bell, 9 goals for Tranmere Rovers on Boxing Day 1935; and Joe Payne for Luton Town, Easter 1936, 10 goals, which also remains the all-time record in English league football for most goals scored in a single match.

I wished goalscorers to be representative of each decade from the more than 120 seasons of British league football. It was also important not just to include 50 top-flight goalscorers – whether that be from the First Division or the Premier League in England and Scotland. Records document that it is more difficult to score goals consistently over a period of time at the highest level, with only 29 players having scored 200 or more league goals in the very top division of English league football. Not every footballer is able to savour playing on Broadway for all or part of their career, and I hope that by celebrating the players who have in some cases plied their trade in the Second Division/Championship or lower leagues for the majority of their careers, recognition is given to their goalscoring prowess. As far as supporters are concerned, these goalscoring feats and achievements are equally important and remarkable.

Another consideration was to include goalscorers from overseas, outside of the British Isles. As far back as 1951/52, Chilean George Robledo scored the winner for Newcastle United in the FA Cup Final versus Arsenal and was also the First Division top scorer in the same season with 33 league goals. Indeed, later in the book you shall read about a goalscorer among the 50 who even predates this time. From around a dozen foreign stars in season 1979/80, the imports have increased whereby, season on season, the goal scoring charts are dominated by the talents of players from Africa, Europe and South America. As overseas players have enhanced and influenced our game at home, I decided to include goalscorers from outside these shores.

I had to omit gifted footballers like Dennis Bergkamp, Eric Cantona and Gianfranco Zola, who have not been as prolific in front of goal, but are heralded as all-time greats of the Premier League era and whose undoubted supreme ability is universally appreciated. They have scored their fair share and have created many more for those around them, but it would have been unfair to include this trio, thus omitting more regular goalscorers. Someone who is and continues to be more than a regular goalscorer is Cristiano Ronaldo, who has amassed over 750 career goals. Ronaldo hit 84 Premier League goals for Manchester United in his first spell at the club and is sure to add to his total the second time around. Judging by records in British football, Ronaldo has not been included because of his tally and length of time in our game, notwithstanding the exceptional numbers he has achieved.

A handful of overseas stars have been selected for our 50. It is always the players that are left out that you feel for in any situation and so, much like substitute benches in the 21st century, there is a growing list of contenders for inclusion. Later in the book, I pay tribute to these goalscorers who have not quite made my starting line-up.

In each section – before our player profiles – I shall also pay tribute to some of the many goalscorers throughout the leagues who have given supporters of all clubs across the United Kingdom so much pleasure over the years. Goals that won leagues and cups at home and abroad, earned European qualification and helped gain promotion or avoid relegation to save a season.

I apologise if your own favourite is not among our lists. I have tried to include and celebrate/highlight as wide a range as possible. The line has been drawn listing forwards who have not been as prolific compared to other front men. These goalscorers have contributed vital goals over their careers (and in many cases are worldwide superstars), but do not find the back of the net as regularly – Mark Hughes, Duncan Ferguson and Peter Crouch would be good examples. Their importance is acknowledged, but I endeavoured that goalscorers who have found the net more often and whom are perhaps less well known are given their moment again under the floodlights, thus the inclusion of some names who maybe are not as familiar to all football followers. Goal scorers come in all sizes, character, personality and from differing backgrounds, each and every one a super-model of design sharing an instinctive ability to find and make time and space enabling the taking of half-chances.

For all our goalscorers this shall be a celebration of the art and joy of goalscoring. I shall touch upon, but not be delving deeply into, the personal lives of our 50 greatest, concentrating more on the goals, the games and the glory.

On a personal note, I would like to mention strikers from my childhood who, although not included in our 50, deserve recognition. Gerry Armstrong – scorer of a memorable winning goal for Northern Ireland versus Spain in World Cup '82. Paul Mariner, Frank Stapleton and Cyrille Regis, whose brilliant hit for WBA featured for many years in the opening credits on *Match of the Day*. Liverpool, Everton and Ipswich ace David Johnson. Chris Garland of Bristol City. Andy Gray, pre-chalkboard, who was a favourite with Villa, Wolves and Everton. Jimmy Greenoff, Dennis Tueart, Lou Macari and Alan Sunderland, famous for a last-minute Cup Final winner. Garry Birtles, Tony Woodcock, and Peter Withe, who scored the goal that won the European Cup for Villa. Paul Goddard and Paul Walsh. Paul Rideout, who netted Wembley winners for England Schoolboys and in the FA Cup Final. Primarily an attacking midfielder, it is impossible not to recognise Norman Whiteside who scored at the World Cup and in both FA Cup and League Cup Finals.

Reminiscing from years gone by, we shall all have our own goalscoring memories from playground to playing fields, through radio, television and going to the match, shared with family, friends and fellow supporters. I hope you are reminded of some of your own in the pages that follow.

In Remembrance:

Ibrox, 5 April 1902

Burnden Park, 9 March 1946

Munich Air Disaster, 6 February 1958

Ibrox Stadium. 2 January 1971

Valley Parade, Bradford City. 11 May 1985

Heysel. 29 May 1985

Hillsborough. 15 April 1989

Founding and Inter-War Years

Forwards were given encouragement in their quest for goals with three new changes in the Laws of the Game. From 1912, goalkeepers were not permitted to handle the ball outside the penalty area. 1925 saw a new advantageous offside law whereby only two players (previously three players) had to be nearer the goal than the attacker, and from 1929 goalkeepers were compelled to stand on their goal line when a penalty kick was taken.

With 86 clubs now split into four divisions, including the newly-formed Division 3 (North) and Division 3 (South), goalscorers were key in issues of promotion and relegation.

Goalscorers of the time included:

'Happy' Harry Hampton, pre-World War I, and Billy Walker, between the wars, joint record scorers for Aston Villa with 213 League goals apiece. 'Happy' Harry also scored both goals in the 1905 Cup Final.

Joe Bradford at Midland rivals Birmingham City scored a club record 249 League goals.

At Blackpool, Jimmy Hampson scored 252 times for the Seasiders, whilst at another seaside town, AFC Bournemouth, who had been elected to Division 3 (South) in 1923, Ron Eyre scored freely for 202 League goals, a club record to this day.

Arthur Chandler hit a record 262 League goals for Leicester City – the majority in Division One from 1923 to 1935.

Inside forward Horatio 'Raich' Carter, 216 league goals. Captained Sunderland to the league title and FA Cup, scoring in the 1937 final.

Henry Cursham, all-time record FA Cup goalscorer with 48 goals in the competition proper for Notts County in the 1870s and 1880s.

In Steel City Sheffield, Harry Johnson of United and Andy Wilson of Wednesday both scored over 200 goals respectively.

Welsh international Ernest Matthew 'Pat' Glover remains Grimsby Town's record scorer with 196 goals.

In the 1920s and 1930s Harry Morris scored 216 League goals for Swindon Town, all in Division 3 (South).

Tom Keetley – 180 League goals in 231 games for Doncaster Rovers in Division 3 (North) – had three brothers play for 'Donny'. Tom also scored 94 league goals in 103 games for Notts County.

Ted Harper – one time record First Division scorer for a season in 1925/26 with 43 league goals for Blackburn Rovers. Also prolific for Preston North End.

Peter Doherty – top scorer as Manchester City won their first league title in 1936/37 and a goalscorer in the final as Derby County won the 1946 FA Cup. Led Northern Ireland to 1958 World Cup Finals as manager.

Jimmy Dunne of the Republic of Ireland holds the English top-flight record of scoring in 12 consecutive league games, doing so for Sheffield United in season 1931/32.

George 'Bomber' Brown, whose goals helped Huddersfield Town make history, winning three consecutive First Division titles in the 1920s, with over 250 career goals.

Between the wars, both with over 300 league goals, Harry Bedford, Blackpool and Derby County, and Harry Johnson, Sheffield United and Mansfield Town.

Jack Southworth was twice Division 1 top scorer, reported to have netted 133 goals in 139 games in the late 1880s and early 1890s before injury and illness ended his career.

Sunderland's Scottish goalscorer John Campbell is one of only seven players to be English top-flight leading scorer on three or more occasions: 1891-92, 1892-93 and 1894-95.

Joe Smith scored 243 league goals for Bolton Wanderers, winning the FA Cup in 1923 and 1926. He then managed Blackpool to cup glory in the 1953 final versus Bolton.

Thomas Waring, known as Tom, nicknamed 'Pongo', over 200 career goals, including 167 for Aston Villa from 1928 to 1935.

Vivian Woodward, England captain with 29 international goals in 23 appearances, also captained British Olympic team to Gold at the 1908 and 1912 Games.

North of the border, during the 'Golden Age of Goalscoring', several players endeavoured to keep up with the legendary Jimmy McGrory of Celtic. Bobby Skinner, 55 league goals in season 1925/26 for Dunfermline; Jimmy Smith of Ayr United, 66 league goals in season 1927/28; and Willie MacFayden, 52 league goals in 1931/32 for Motherwell.

Steve Bloomer

The goal standard set by the first superstar of football was so high that over the next 100 years all subsequent goalscorers who followed have found it nigh on impossible to match or eclipse.

Steve Bloomer dealt in goals, although in the 19th century newspaper reporters did not always consider it necessary to name the actual goalscorer. Bloomer himself knew the score and was devoted to goalscoring.

He was the original of only seven players to so far hit 350 or more league goals in the English and Scottish Leagues – 352 in 598 League appearances, displaying remarkable durability over 22 seasons of league football.

While working alongside his father at the forge, playing for local side

Derby Swifts, he scored 14 goals in a single game and was signed as an amateur by Derby County, then as a professional, initially earning 37½ pence a week.

As a founder member of the league in 1888, he had joined an established side and made his debut for Derby County in 1892.

Slight in build and nicknamed 'Paleface' because of his complexion and 'Destroying Angel' for his devastating finishing, with his natural all-round sporting ability as a useful cricketer and baseball player, aligned with a two-footed footballing prowess, he soon flourished at football league level.

In September 1895, Bloomer scored both Derby goals in a 2-0 win versus Sunderland in their first home match as full tenants at the Baseball Ground. Before that the club had been playing their games at the County Cricket Ground.

In two spells with the Rams, he scored 332 goals in 525 appearances, with 291 in the league from 473 appearances, including 17 league hat-tricks – with a double hat-trick in a 9-0 victory versus Sheffield Wednesday in January 1899. He was the First Division top scorer a record five times for a single club: 1895-96, 1896-97, 1898-99, 1900-01 and 1903-04. Uniquely, he is the one player in the history of top-flight English football to be a season's outright top scorer in two separate centuries.

Major silverware eluded Bloomer as Derby were league runners-up in season 1895/96 and were defeated in three FA Cup Finals, with Steve scoring in the 1898 final played at the Crystal Palace versus Nottingham Forest.

The football world was stunned when big spending Middlesbrough signed Bloomer in 1906 (the previous year they had paid the first £1,000 transfer fee for Alf Common). In his first season on Teesside, he scored four at Woolwich Arsenal in a 5-3 away win. In total with Boro there were 61 First Division goals in 125 appearances.

On his return to Derby in 1910 he was given a hero's welcome, brass band and all, at the Baseball Ground, helping the club win promotion back to the First Division as Second Division Champions in 1911/12.

Bloomer's devotion to goalscoring was rewarded with 314 top-flight league goals, placing him second on the all-time list, from starting out as a teenager to playing 11 days beyond his 40th birthday in January 1914.

For England over 12 years from 1895 to 1907, he was just as prolific, scoring 28 goals in 23 international appearances (all competitive fixtures) including in a record ten consecutive matches from debut v Ireland in 1895. At Cardiff in 1896, he hit five goals versus Wales in a 9-1 victory. In February 1899, he scored twice at Roker Park in a 13-2 win versus Ireland – still the record number of goals scored by England in a single match. He holds the record of most goals by an England player in matches against the auld enemy Scotland with eight.

Upon retirement, he left Derby to coach in Germany with Britannia Berlin 92, where, with the outbreak of World War I, he was held captive in a civilian camp at Ruhleben in Berlin from August 1914 to his release in March 1918. Football really was a matter of life and death for Bloomer and his fellow inmates. Through playing in the camp, he later recalled, "Myself and many others would not have survived without football."

He then coached in Holland and Spain and served his beloved Derby County.

While in Spain he managed Real Union, winning the Copa del Rey in 1924 beating Real Madrid in the final. Since 2017, Derby and the Basque club have played for the Steve Bloomer Trophy in honour of the connection they share with the great man.

Steve Bloomer, goalscoring pioneer, really was ahead of his time, endorsing football kit including 'the boot that never fails to score'.

To this day at Pride Park, the club anthem *Steve Bloomer's Watchin'* is played before each home match with a statue of Steve overlooking the pitch.

He was born in 1874, the same year as the great American writer Robert Frost, whose works include *The Lone Striker*, poignantly appropriate as Steve Bloomer was quite literally in a league of his own.

George Camsell

1926/27 – a sign of the times. Naturalist David Attenborough and creator of Paddington Bear Michael Bond are born. The original 'It Girl' Clara Bow stars in one of the major silent movies as talking pictures ('talkies') usher in a new era of cinema. In the world of sport, golf's inaugural Ryder Cup takes place and future Tarzan, Johnny Weissmuller, sets new swimming records. Football sees George Camsell score a then record 59 League goals for Middlesbrough FC in the Second Division, overtaking Jimmy Cookson's 44 goals for Chesterfield in the previous season 1925/26 in Third Division (North).

Cup finals are named after footballers. Well, the 1926/27 season should be known as 'The George Camsell Season'. Recently signed by Middlesbrough, Camsell was only called up to the first team after regular centre-forward Jimmy McClelland was injured and he grabbed his opportunity with both feet and head.

He did not score in his first game of the season but then went on an unprecedented run of goalscoring. In the next 24 league games he scored 47 goals, including a sequence of scoring in 12 consecutive matches with 29 goals. Over the festive period he was unplayable, with four goals in the 7-1 win over Swansea and all five in a 5-3 victory over Manchester City on Christmas Day 1926.

Camsell created a new league goalscoring high by late February and ultimately raised the bar to new heights with 59 League goals in 37 appearances come the end of the season. He also scored five goals in the FA Cup, giving him a total of 64 league and cup goals for the campaign.

Modestly, George revealed the secrets of his success: "My goal secrets? Get off the mark quickly, go all out for goal when the chance comes, and do not be discouraged by shots that go wide. Keep on trying. Have faith in yourself and never be afraid of 'having a go' for goal."

Sound advice from a master goalscorer, as the record tally won Boro the 1926/27 Second Division Championship and remains the highest individual number of goals scored in the second tier of English football. He also scored nine league hat-tricks during the season, a record for any division in the history of English football.

The following season (1927/28), he became the first player in the history of English football to score a century of goals in consecutive seasons, with 37 goals – 33 in the First Division – including all his side's goals in a 4-2 victory over Dixie Dean's Everton at Ayresome Park in September 1927 and four in the FA Cup. 101 goals in two seasons! Camsell's goalscoring is even more extraordinary considering Middlesbrough finished bottom of the First Division table in 1927/28.

The following season he scored 30 league goals as Boro again won the Second Division Championship. Back in the top flight he scored 29 league goals in 34 First Division appearances in 1929/30. In season 1930/31 he scored 32 league goals and in season 1933/34 he hit four in a record 10-3 victory versus Sunderland. In 1935/36 he went one better, with five goals versus Aston Villa in September 1935.

Before his time in the sunshine, he worked underground as a miner and played locally for Durham Chapel, Tow Law Town and Esh Winning. He joined home town club Durham City, then a Third Division (North) League side.

Scoring 20 goals in 21 League appearances for Durham City caught the eye of Teesside neighbours Middlesbrough who signed Camsell in 1925. Over 14 seasons at Ayresome Park he would create a lasting legacy and is among a select group of footballers who hold both the individual season and aggregate goalscoring records at their clubs. The historic 59 league goals season and 325 league goals in 419 appearances for Boro including 233 in the top-flight, placing him 13th on the all-time list of top-flight goalscorers. In total there were 345 goals in league and cup from 453 appearances.

Quite typically, in his 37th year he signed off with a goal in his final game for Middlesbrough in April 1939 in a 3-2 win over Leicester City.

His exploits with England were just as extraordinary, scoring in all nine of his internationals, hitting 18 goals in total. He scored twice on his international debut in a 4-1 win in Paris versus France in May 1929. He hit four versus Belgium in Brussels in May 1929 in a 5-1 away win and a hat-trick at Stamford Bridge versus Wales in a 6-0 win in November 1929. In December 1935 he scored a double versus Germany in a 3-0 England win at White Hart Lane.

During the war years George worked for factories on Teesside before becoming scout, coach and assistant secretary at Middlesbrough FC. As a scout he discovered a young forward called Brian Clough who said, "George was reputed to be the bravest centre-forward in the whole football league."

Upon retiring from Middlesbrough in 1960, the club rewarded his loyal service with the gift of a television. After football he enjoyed bowls, tennis and snooker. He was deserving of a statue, particularly for the 1926/27 'George Camsell season'.

Dixie Dean

William Ralph Dean, Bill, Dixie, Dixie Dean – the very name conjures up images of an almost mythical goalscoring character from the pages of a comic book. For sure though, he was real, as testified by thousands of Evertonians flocking to Goodison Park to witness goalscoring feats that would endure and ensure immortality status.

That status is due in part to the extraordinary goalscoring spree of season 1927/28. The previous campaign George Camsell had established a new high of 59 league goals. Dixie went one better – a record to this day that shall probably never be topped.

Including a hat-trick versus Liverpool at Anfield on Merseyside derby day, he scored a stunning 60 league goals in 39 First Division games as Everton won the League Championship with the team recording 102 league goals in total. Dean also scored all five versus Manchester United in a 5-2 win and a hat-trick versus Leicester in a 7-1 success.

Going into the last two games of the season, he was on 53 league goals. Away to Burnley he scored four in a 5-3 victory and hit a hat-trick in a 3-3 draw with Arsenal at Goodison Park to clinch the record and celebrate Everton as champions.

During the season, he scored 82 goals in total – another record, 60 league, three FA Cup, six Inter-League, eight international trials and five international goals. He is the one player in English football to record 60 league goals in a season; the next highest in top-flight history is Tom 'Pongo' Waring for Aston Villa in 1930/31 with 49 league goals.

Dixie Dean began his professional career across the Mersey with Tranmere Rovers in Division Three (North). After scoring 27 league goals in 29 games, he moved to Everton in March 1925 for £3,000 to begin a lifelong love affair with the Blues.

Nicknamed Dixie because of his thick jet-black curly hair, he preferred friends to call him Bill. In June 1926 he was involved in a serious motorcycle accident, saving his lady friend. Dixie suffered a fractured skull, broken cheekbone and fractured jaw in two places. Miraculously, he recovered and was playing and scoring goals again by the autumn, completing the 1926/27 season with 21 league goals from 27 appearances.

With Everton he would score 383 goals in 433 games, including 349 in the league – 310 of those in the top flight, both league records for a player at a single English league club.

Despite his goalscoring feats, just two seasons after being crowned

Champions of England, Everton were relegated for the first time in club history in season 1929/30.

Immediately they bounced back as Division 2 Champions with Dixie leading the way as top scorer with 39 league goals including four versus Plymouth Argyle in a club record equalling league 9-1 victory. The following season, Everton truly were back, winning the league in 1931/32 and once again he was the division's top scorer with 45 league goals, including two bunch of fives versus Sheffield Wednesday 9-3 and Chelsea 7-2. He hit Leicester for four in a 9-2 win and grabbed another Merseyside derby hat-trick versus Liverpool in a 3-1 triumph at Anfield.

Further success followed the next season as Everton reached their first Wembley cup final in 1933. For the first time in a FA Cup final, players would be numbered (1-22) with Dixie wearing number 9. As fellow finalist Manchester City also wore blue jerseys, it was decided both teams would have neutral colours, Everton white and City red. Whatever the colours, as per usual Dixie found the net in a 3-0 victory and Captain Dean, making what would prove to be his one and only cup final appearance, proudly lifted the trophy from the Duke of York.

While at Goodison he won 18 England caps, scoring 16 international goals with two hat-tricks in 1927, both away from home versus Belgium (9-1) and Luxembourg (5-2). The same year, in a historic (2-1) win, he netted both versus Scotland at Hampden Park, the first England victory in Glasgow since 1904. He also scored twice in Paris versus France (6-0) and an international goal at Goodison versus Ireland in October 1928 when England won 2-1.

Even for immortals like Dixie, playing is temporary and in March 1938 he left Everton. It is worth noting that the 349 league goals were scored in only 399 appearances!

After brief spells with Notts County in Division 3 (South) and Sligo Rovers in the League of Ireland, Dixie retired as injury and the outbreak of World War II overtook all events. Throughout his football league career he was never booked and never sent off.

He continued to play in charity matches and also Everton versus Liverpool veterans' games as the star attraction.

Dean was a true working-class hero who used to catch the train and tram from his home in Birkenhead on match day. He was a caretaker/watchman with Littlewoods and servant of the British Army on the Home Front.

Dixie Dean's footballing career could easily be defined and measured by facts and figures such as 200 league goals after 199 games, a record 37 league hat-tricks and 379 league goals in 437 appearances for Tranmere, Everton and Notts County, but his legacy, cemented by a statue at Everton commemorating his goalscoring, will last forever because of friendships forged including with legendary Liverpool goalkeeper Elisha Scott, with whom he had many a duel, and the lasting impression he made on supporters.

Named after the goalscoring great, Liverpool is home to the Dixie Dean Hotel. If you want to read more about the great Evertonian, *Dixie Dean: The Inside Story of a Football Icon* by John Keith is highly recommended. In March 1980, while attending a Merseyside derby at his beloved Goodison Park, Bill departed Everton FC for Heaven FC.

Ted Drake

The first time I knew of Ted Drake was from a soccer card collection where Ted was featured in the all-time greats section of the album.

The cards, similar to football cigarette cards issued around wartime, gave a description of a brave centre-forward of the 1930s and listed his achievements on the reverse side. On the picture card side, this old-time footballer had a slicked back tidy hairstyle with a high buttoned football shirt collar.

Since then I have realised the greatness of Edward Joseph Drake's achievements. He had the distinction of being leading marksman in the First Division, scoring the winner in the FA Cup Final and finding the net seven times in a league match, all within the space of a year.

Growing up kicking a ball around the back streets, he dreamed of emulating his hero, Southampton and England centre-forward Bill Rawlings. After impressing with local side Winchester City, Southampton manager George Kay signed up Ted for the Saints junior side, continuing his day job as a gas meter inspector until signing professional terms in November 1931.

He soon blossomed in the first

team, displaying characteristic bravery, determination and a talent for shooting with either foot, while also playing county cricket in the summer for Hampshire. Arsenal made an approach to sign him, but he wished to remain on the south coast with his home town club.

During the Second Division season of 1933/34, with Drake scoring 22 league goals in 27 appearances, the Gunners once again came calling. With Southampton in debt the club accepted a £6,000 fee and he left Hampshire for Highbury in March 1934 after 47 league goals in 71 appearances.

Arsenal manager George Allison, who had been appointed following the death of Herbert Chapman, said Ted was "the best centre-forward in the world". Joining the champions of England, he soon repaid the faith placed in him. In his first full season, 1934/35, he scored a club record 42 league goals, including four times hitting four goals in a game: Birmingham City (5-1), Chelsea away (5-2), Wolves (7-0) and Middlesbrough (8-0). He also scored a hat-trick in Arsenal's record home victory versus Spurs in October 1934 (5-1) and a double in Arsenal's biggest North London derby victory, 6-0 at White Hart Lane in March 1935. He was the First Division top scorer as Arsenal won the third of three consecutive league titles.

The following season, on 14th December 1935 at Villa Park, he scored seven goals against Aston Villa, becoming the first player to do so in a top-flight match (a record that remains to this day in the history of English football). The scoreline was 7-1. It could have been an outright record eight, as he hit the crossbar with one effort. What made Drake's magnificent seven all the more remarkable was that he had only recently recovered from a cartilage operation.

Wembley glory followed as he scored the only goal of the game when Arsenal beat Sheffield United to win the 1936 FA Cup, where once again he displayed his renowned courage, playing with a bandaged and injured knee, and two seasons later in 1937/38 there was another league title for the team of the decade.

On Drake's England debut in November 1934, when a record seven Arsenal players lined up to play World Cup winners Italy, he scored the winner in a 3-2 victory in a bruising encounter remembered as 'The Battle of Highbury'; in Italy the game is known as 'The Lions of Highbury'.

Drake scored six goals in five international appearances and was the first player to hit a hat-trick in a full England international on their own home ground, doing so versus Hungary at Highbury in December 1936.

Up to the beginning of the Second World War before his 27th birthday, Drake had for Arsenal scored 123 league goals in 168 appearances with 136 goals in 182 games in all competitions. For the Saints and the Gunners he had a total of 170 league goals in 239 league appearances.

During the war he served with the RAF and represented and featured in war-time fixtures. A recurring spinal injury ended his football career before peacetime matches resumed, so stopping a prolific goalscoring run in its tracks.

Ted went into management with Hendon and Reading. With Reading he guided the club to second place in Division 3 (South). He was then appointed manager of Chelsea. In season 1954/55 'Drake's Ducklings' became the first Chelsea side to win the League Championship. In doing so he became the first to win the League Championship as both a player and a manager. He also took young forwards Bobby Smith and Jimmy Greaves under his wing.

After disagreements with Chelsea, Drake and the club parted company. He was a bookmaker for a time, returning to the game as assistant manager with Fulham and then Barcelona. Out of football once more he was an insurance salesman before returning to Craven Cottage in charge of the reserves and as chief scout before being made Life President of Fulham Football Club in 1975.

Ted had been Heaven sent from Hampshire, often playing through the pain barrier, his goalscoring record earning his place in any collection of all-time greats.

Hughie Gallacher

On the pitch between the wars, Hugh Kilpatrick Gallacher was a confident, dynamic, outstanding centre-forward. Off the field he was similarly stylish, his attire like a character from a Jimmy Cagney film.

He was generous but his independent temperamental spirit would often land him in hot water as he was frequently sent off and was involved in personal controversial away from football. Remember him this way... as a glorious goalscorer – 463 goals in 624 career matches, 387 league goals in 541 appearances in Scotland and England and 296 English League goals in 430 appearances, including 246 in the top flight.

Where did all these goals come from?

Gallacher started playing for local side Bellshill Athletic before joining the then non-league side Queen of the South, scoring 18 goals in his first seven games.

While recovering from double pneumonia (he had worked on munitions during the war and down the mine) he signed for Airdrieonians in May 1921. He was to the forefront of the most wonderful time in the history of Airdrie FC, scoring 100 goals in 129 league and cup appearances for the Diamonds as the club finished runners-up in the Scottish top flight for four consecutive seasons (Hughie playing in three) and won the Scottish Cup in 1924 for the first and, to date, only time.

The scouts from England were taking note and, aged 22, Gallacher joined Newcastle United for a club record fee of £6,500 in December 1925. On his debut versus Everton, he made an immediate impact, as he and Dixie Dean both scored in a 3-3 draw. Later, Bill Dean recalled, "He was the finest centre-forward I've ever seen... He had brilliant ball control, the heart of a lion... and complete and utter confidence in his ability."

On Tyneside and as captain in the 1926/27 season, he inspired the Geordies to what is still their most recent League Championship in the top flight. As always, leading from the front with a club record 36 league goals denying Huddersfield Town a historic fourth title in a row. His tally included all four goals versus Aston Villa in a 4-0 win and hat-tricks in comprehensive victories against Everton 7-3 and Arsenal 6-1, plus the only goal of the game in the Tyne-Wear derby versus Sunderland.

In season 1928/29 he scored 24 goals in 34 games, including a hat-trick away at Manchester City in a 4-2 win. In 1929/30 he scored 29 league goals, with a home hat-trick against the red half of Manchester, beating United 4-1.

After five seasons he had scored 143 goals in 174 appearances for the Magpies with 133 coming in the league. Against his wishes Gallacher was sold to Chelsea for £10,000. In September 1930, with his newly-promoted club, he returned to St. James Park as a visiting player and received a hero's welcome from a record crowd of 68,386, stating, "The reception I got today was the highlight of my career."

He was quoted as saying, "I don't like London, I can't get used to the climate." The weather certainly did not disagree with his goalscoring as he hit 72 goals in 132 appearances for the Blues. Among his Chelsea goals was one in the 1932 FA Cup semi-final in a 2-1 defeat to Newcastle; a month later in the league he scored a hat-trick versus his former club in a 4-1 victory at Stamford Bridge.

In November 1934, he moved again, signing for Derby County where he scored a further 38 First Division goals in 51 games, helping the Rams to runners-up spot behind Sunderland in 1935/36.

After spells with Notts County in Division 3 (South), again as captain, and Grimsby Town where his goals kept them in the top flight, Gallacher had his swansong season back in the North East. In his final season of league football in 1938/39, he scored 18 league goals in 31 games for Gateshead in Division 3 (North), boosting attendances wherever he played.

On returning to Tyneside, he said, "My heart has been here ever since I left United eight years ago, I intend to spend the rest of my life with my adopted folk in Gateshead." That he did, including for a time working in sports journalism.

For his native Scotland, Gallacher is the 3rd highest scorer of all time, despite playing in an era when there were fewer international fixtures. He netted 23 international goals from 20 appearances and in April 1925 he scored both Scotland goals in a 2-0 victory versus England at Hampden Park. He was also part of the Wembley Wizards team in 1928 that defeated England 5-1 when he was playing his first game back after serving a two-month suspension for pushing a referee into a bath. Even more astonishing than that, he didn't score any of the goals. He made up for that the following year by scoring a record four in a 7-3 victory over Northern Ireland in Belfast. He also hit a hat-trick versus Wales in a 4-2 win and both Scotland goals in a 2-0 away win in France.

During the war he played and perhaps ironically refereed charity matches. Reflecting on his love of the game. Hughie said, "Lay on the transport, find some size six boots, and leave the rest to me."

David Halliday

Also known as Dave Halliday – either way he is the unknown goalscorer, who deserves much greater acclaim for his ability to find the way to goal. Between the wars, Halliday's playing achievements are incredible, even among the elite all-time greats of goalscoring and such feats should be recognised and remembered.

He is the fastest in history to reach 100 English top-flight league goals, doing so in only 101 games whilst at Sunderland AFC. Of the 29 players to have scored 200 or more league goals in England's top division, only Dixie Dean did at a quicker rate, Halliday's 211 coming from 246 games in only eight seasons.

It is reasonable to suggest he is arguably the most lethal finisher in British football history. 365 goals in 488 games – 3 goals every 4 games. He is the only player in the top-flight history of English football to score 30 plus league goals in four consecutive seasons: 1925/26, 1926/27, 1927/28 and 1928/29 (all for Sunderland).

He is unique among goalscorers, holding the distinction of being the outright top scorer in a season for clubs in both the Scottish and English top flights, Dundee and Sunderland respectively.

That makes it all the more inconceivable that he was never capped by Scotland at full international level, even taking into account that he played in an era alongside Hughie Gallacher and Jimmy McGrory.

As a budding goalscorer he played with local Dumfries side, Queen of the South, then a non-league side, as he was employed with the car manufacturer Arrol-Johnston. Scoring at a goal a game, St. Mirren offered him senior football in 1920 and he agreed on the condition he could continue his engineering and travel to Paisley on match days.

Still a teenager, he became a full-time footballer when he moved to Dundee. Quite tall for a player of his time in the 1920s at just under 6 feet, he was known as 'Big Davie'.

In four seasons with Dundee, he notched 90 league goals in 126 appearances including top scoring with 38 league goals in season 1923/24 ahead of the likes of Gallacher and McGrory. The next season he was top scorer in the club's cup run as Dundee reached only their second ever Scottish Cup Final – losing 2-1 to Celtic.

In the summer of 1925 Dundee could not refuse the offer of £4,000 from Sunderland and Halliday was on his way to Wearside. Incredibly, his strike rate rose: 165 goals in 175 league and cup games with that record 100 league goals from 101 league games and First Division top scorer with 43 goals in 1928/29.

In November 1929, the most famous club and manager in the land came calling. Arsenal and Herbert Chapman were building a dynasty and signed Halliday for £6,500.

With Arsenal, Halliday was involved in the historic 6-6 high scoring draw (the first in English league football), hitting four goals v Leicester City on Easter Monday 1930. Despite this, a few weeks later he was not included in the Cup Final eleven and left Highbury with a goals record of played 15, goals 8.

Joining Manchester City in November 1930, Halliday continued his goalscoring spree with 32 league goals in 45 appearances, but once again he suffered Cup Final heartache when not selected for the 1933 final.

Having just turned 32, he moved on again in December 1933 to Division 3 (South) side Clapton Orient, weighing in with 32 goals in 56 league and cup appearances.

In June 1935 he was appointed player/manager of Yeovil Town and scored a further three goals in the FA Cup, taking his career league and cup tally to 368 goals.

Whilst on overseas tours with Dundee in the 1920s, he found the net versus Athletic Bilbao, Barcelona, Real Madrid and Valencia, demonstrating his ability that, given a chance, he could find the net against any opposition in any situation.

In the 1937/38 season he returned to his homeland when he accepted the post of manager of Aberdeen. As on the playing field, Dave Halliday created history in management. He led the Dons to their first ever successes in both the Scottish Cup in 1947 and the Scottish League title in 1954/55. At Leicester City, with goalscorer Arthur Rowley, Halliday managed the Foxes to the 1956/57 Second Division Championship.

As a person, David Halliday was regarded as a gentleman and as someone with great personal integrity. Likewise, as a footballer, he should be held up as a goalscoring example of the very highest calibre.

Gordon Hodgson

In the history of Liverpool Football Club and among all its great goalscorers, Gordon Hodgson heads the list with the most top-flight goals for the Reds: 233 in 358 league appearances across a decade from 1925/26 to 1935/36.

He was the first and one of only three Liverpool players (alongside Roger Hunt and Ian Rush) to score 20 or more goals in five consecutive seasons (1930/31 to 1934/35).

With 288 First Division goals in total, he is 4th on the all-time list of top-flight goalscorers in the history of English Football, only behind Jimmy Greaves, Steve Bloomer and Dixie Dean and above the likes of Alan Shearer, Rush and Denis Law.

Born in Johannesburg to English parents, Hodgson's goalscoring feats also see him top the list of overseas goalscorers in British football history – more than modern day strikers Thierry Henry, Sergio Aguero and Henrik Larsson.

As part of the South African side touring Europe including England, Hodgson's Springboks beat Liverpool 5-2 and Everton 3-1. At the time the *Liverpool Echo* reported on the attractive nature of the visitors play and "the inside right, who took the eye from the first moment."

Liverpool were building a contingent of South African players that would include among their ranks goalkeeper Arthur Riley and winger Berry 'Nivvy' Nieuwenhuys and signed Hodgson in December 1925 from Transvaal FC, having previously represented Benoni, Rustenbury and Pretoria in his native land.

His goalscoring exploits are all the more admirable considering that during his stay on Merseyside Liverpool were a mid-table side and did not advance beyond the quarter-finals of the FA Cup.

The club's highest finish in the league in his time at Anfield was in season 1928/29, finishing 5th in the First Division. In that season, Hodgson scored 30 league goals including a hat-trick in a club record 8-0 home win versus Burnley. He also scored a hat-trick in a 4-4 draw with Arsenal at Highbury.

In 1930/31, even as the Reds finished 9th in the table, Hodgson scored 36 league goals – a record which still stands as the greatest haul by a player in Liverpool's history for a single season in the top flight of English football. This included three hat-tricks at Anfield: Chelsea 3-1, Sheffield United 6-1 and Blackpool 5-2 and a four-goal blast away at Sheffield Wednesday in a 5-3 win.

At the height of his popularity a local biscuit seller would call out "Hodgson's Choice, Hodgson's Choice" on match days at Anfield, for his home-made ginger nuts – five for a penny!

In the 1933/34 season, he scored hat-tricks in consecutive home league games at Anfield in March 1934, Middlesbrough 6-2 and all four versus Birmingham City 4-1, among a total of 24 league goals for the season.

Even as Liverpudlians endured a barren trophyless spell in the shadow of their neighbours Everton, they could console themselves that they had a goalscorer of such stature that he could be compared to Dixie Dean. In season 1934/35 at Anfield, Hodgson scored both the Reds goals in a 2-1 win (Dixie scored for the Blues).

In Hodgson's final season on Merseyside, he further emphasised the fact by scoring twice on derby day as the Reds recorded their biggest win in history against their local rivals in September 1935, beating the Blues 6-0 at Anfield. For the record, Hodgson also scored the winner at Goodison Park, 2-1 in the FA Cup Third Round in January 1932.

For service to Liverpool Football Club, Gordon was rewarded with a benefit of £650. In January 1936, he joined Aston Villa, scoring 11 league goals, including 4 in the top-flight, before moving to Yorkshire with Leeds United.

As devastating in front of goal as ever, he scored a further 51 First Division goals in 81 appearances, including five in an 8-2 win over Leicester City in October 1938. He also scored against Liverpool for Leeds at both Anfield and Elland Road.

Hodgson was a dual international, capped by both England and South Africa, and also represented the Football League. He won three England caps, all in the 1930/31 season, scoring once versus Wales in a 4-0 victory at the Racecourse Ground, Wrexham.

During wartime he guested for Hartlepool United and York City.

A tall, strong looking forward who rarely missed a game, he also enjoyed baseball and excelled at cricket, playing 56 first class matches for Lancashire, taking 148 wickets as a fast bowler.

After the war he became manager of Third Division (S) side Port Vale and when the manager of Liverpool George Kay retired in January 1951, Gordon was among those interviewed for the vacant post.

Although this was not too be, through his illustrious playing career, especially on Merseyside, Hodgson was taken into the hearts of Liverpudlians as one of their own – an adopted goalscoring 'Springkop'.

David Jack

With the wonderful full name of David Bone Nightingale Jack, the Nightingale is his mother's name, the Bone – nobody seems to know. One thing is for sure, when it came to goalscoring, Jack was a King!

The first goalscorer in a Wembley FA Cup final, the first five-figure £10,000 footballer, the first and one of only three players alongside Jimmy Greaves and Alan Shearer with 100 top-flight league goals in English football history with two separate clubs and 7th on the all-time list with 257 top-flight league goals.

Bolton born, he grew up on the south and east coasts of Plymouth and Southend, where his father Bob managed both clubs.

After progressing through the junior teams at Argyle with the outbreak of the First World War he served with the Royal Navy and also played for the Navy team and guested for Chelsea.

After the war he returned to play for Plymouth in the Southern League. In 1920, he was in the starting XI for Argyle's first ever match in the Football League versus Norwich City in the first season of the newly-formed Third Division.

In December 1920, he was signed by his home town club Bolton Wanderers for £3,500. With Plymouth he scored 15 goals in all competitions from 48 appearances, including three football league goals from 14 appearances. Joining midway through the 1920/21 season he helped Wanderers to third place in the league, developing a lethal partnership with Joe Smith.

In season 1922/23, Jack scored all of Bolton's goals in a cup run of 1-0 wins, including the semi-final winner versus Sheffield United. In the first FA Cup Final to be played at the new Empire Stadium at Wembley, David created history by scoring the first ever Wembley cup final goal in a 2-0 victory over West Ham United. Bolton had won their first FA Cup.

In 1924/25, with 26 league goals, he was the First Division's second top scorer behind Frank Roberts of Manchester City as Bolton again finished third in the league.

In the 1926 FA Cup Final, he scored the only goal of the game to become the first player to score in two Wembley cup finals as Bolton won the cup for a second time, beating City one nil.

In October 1928, aged 29, he made history once more, as the first five figure transfer in British football history, signed by Herbert Chapman's Arsenal for £10,890. In eight seasons with Bolton, Jack scored 144 league goals in 295 First Division appearances with 161 goals in all competitions.

In his first season at Highbury, he notched 25 goals in 31 appearances. In the 1930 FA Cup semi-final he scored versus Hull City to send Arsenal to the final where the Gunners won the cup for the first time in club history, beating Huddersfield Town.

In 1930/31, Jack scored 31 league goals in 35 appearances, including hat-tricks away to Chelsea (5-1) and at home to Blackpool (7-1), with a four-goal blast versus Grimsby Town (9-1). In April 1931. along with his fellow 'flying forwards' Cliff Bastin and Jack Lambert, he scored in a 3-1 victory versus Liverpool at Highbury to give Arsenal their first league title. The Gunners scored a club record 127 league goals and created a new top-flight record of 66 points (two points for a win). Arsenal had also become the first Southern club to win the First Division (top-flight) league title.

In January 1932, he scored a hat-trick in Arsenal's record cup victory versus Darwen, 11-1 in the Third Round of the FA Cup.

Jack won further League titles in seasons 1932/33 and 1933/34 as Arsenal equalled Huddersfield Town's English league record of three consecutive top-flight championships. With his first team appearances now limited and the signing of Ted Drake, he retired from league football, aged 35, in May 1934.

Arsenal record: 113 league goals in 181 league appearances. 124 goals in total.

With Bolton Wanderers and Arsenal: 257 league goals, all in the top flight, from 476 league appearances.

With England, playing at a time when the side was chosen by committee, he scored three international goals from nine caps (four Bolton, five Arsenal). He made his debut versus Wales in 1924. The goals were against France in Paris (5-1 win), victory over Scotland at Wembley (5-2), the first of four internationals as the England captain, and away to Germany in Berlin (3-3).

Before the Second World War he was manager of Southend United. He then ran a greyhound track in Sunderland. In peacetime he returned to football as manager of Middlesbrough and then with Shelbourne in the League of Ireland.

He joined the Air Ministry as a civil servant and continued to scout for Southend.

Remembered as one of the ornaments of the Golden Age of Football, with perfect poise and body swerve, looking like two players with a ball at each of four feet. A footballer first among equals: D.B.N. Jack.

Tommy Lawton

In *Football Monthly* magazine, prior to the start of the Premier League in August 1992, Tom Finney named his Top 10 strikers. "Tommy Lawton was the best centre-forward I ever saw. He used his height to maximum effort to dominate in the air, and was superb on the ground as well. He was a tremendous goalscorer. I put Greaves second to Lawton in my list of best British strikers, Greaves was the most lethal finisher of any era."

Still only 13½ years old, Tommy Lawton displayed his wonderful goalscoring ability from an early age, scoring twice for Bolton Schoolboys in a 3-2 defeat versus their Liverpool counterparts at Goodison Park in March 1933.

After interest from home town club Bolton Wanderers and Sheffield Wednesday, Lawton signed as an amateur for Burnley. While waiting to come of age to sign professional terms he worked as the club's office boy.

He made his Burnley debut versus Doncaster Rovers in March 1936, aged 16 years 174 days (at the time the youngest ever centre-forward to appear in the Football League). On turning 17, he signed as a professional and was on £7 a week with a £2 win bonus. Four days after his 17th birthday in October 1936, he scored a hat-trick versus Spurs in a Second Division match at Turf Moor.

After 16 goals in 25 league appearances for the Clarets, Everton signed Lawton on New Year's Eve 1936 for £6,500. He was to replace the legendary Dixie Dean, an almost impossible task to emulate the great man. The pair appeared together for the first time in a FA Cup defeat to Spurs with both master and prodigy finding the net.

As Dixie finished his Everton career, Lawton, while still a teenager, rose to the challenge by topping the First Division goalscoring charts in consecutive seasons: 1937/38 with 28 goals, including scoring in both Merseyside derbies; and 1938/39 with 34 goals, including a double at Anfield in a 3-0 Everton victory – the second season of which saw Everton win the League title.

The 1939/40 season began as usual and after three league games, reigning champions Everton had 3 points and 5 goals – all scored by Tommy Lawton. Then, on 3rd September 1939, war broke out and the football league programme was abandoned and the competition did not resume until season 1946/47. Like everyone else who had found the net in the new campaign, Tommy's goals were removed from the records. Still a month short of his 20th birthday, the war interrupted Lawton's career.

During the war, he served in the Army as a physical instructor. On Christmas Day 1940, he played in both the Merseyside derby and for Tranmere Rovers v Crewe, scoring twice in a 2-2 draw. He also guested for Leicester City, Aldershot Town and his parent club Everton, hitting over 150 war-time goals.

In November 1945, for a record fee of £11,500, Lawton joined Chelsea, leaving Everton with 65 league goals from 87 appearances. On his Chelsea debut in the club's first 'competitive match' as football resumed after the war, he scored in the FA Cup Third Round versus Leicester City in January 1946. In the league he scored 30 goals in 42 appearances.

Perhaps surprisingly, as he was still England's centre-forward, he agreed to sign for ambitious Third Division Notts County who paid the first £20,000 fee in British football for his services in 1947.

Lawton repaid the fee and then some, with 90 league goals from 151 appearances, including 31 as the division's top scorer in 1949/50 as champions County returned to the second tier of English football for the first time since 1935. During his time at Meadow Lane, he also scored four as the club recorded their biggest league victory of 11-1 versus Newport County in January 1949.

After a couple of seasons with Brentford (17 league goals in 50 appearances), Lawton's swansong was one more shot in the top flight, making his debut for league champions Arsenal in September 1953, scoring in a 3-1 win over Blackpool in the Charity Shield. His record with the Gunners was 13 league goals from 35 appearances.

His goalscoring record overall in league football was 231 league goals from 390 appearances.

At international level for England, he scored 22 goals from 23 caps, including a goal in the match to celebrate the 75th anniversary of the FA with a 3-0 victory versus the Rest of Europe in 1938 at Highbury. He also scored four goals in a match twice, versus Holland in 1946 and Portugal in 1947. He also scored twice for Great Britain versus the Rest of Europe in a 6-1 victory at Hampden Park, Glasgow in May 1947.

There were a further 22 war-time goals, including twice in a charity match in aid of the Red Cross versus Scotland in January 1942 at the Empire Stadium, Wembley.

Now in his 37th year, he was appointed player/manager of non-league Kettering Town in February 1956.

Finding himself in financial difficulties in 1970, he wrote to his friend and long-time Chelsea fan the film maker Richard Attenborough for assistance. Dickie kindly obliged with a cheque for £100.

In 1972, former team mate Joe Mercer organised a testimonial match for Lawton at Goodison Park with guests including Bobbys Moore and Charlton.

The following year he released his acclaimed autobiography, *When the Cheering Stopped*. Like for all former footballers, the cheering may have stopped, but as Tom Finney recalled his number one goalscorer, Tommy Lawton shall never be forgot!

Jimmy McGrory

A goal a game for 15 seasons. Some 100 years after his debut, James Edward McGrory remains the leading goalscorer for a single club in the history of British football, with the remarkable tally of 468 goals from 445 appearances for Celtic Football Club. In the league for Celtic he scored 395 goals in 378 appearances with 73 goals in 67 Scottish Cup games.

Born in Glasgow, the son of Irish immigrants, McGrory's natural footballing talent emerged, earning £2 a week playing for St. Roch's juniors. Signed aged 17 by the first Celtic manager, Willie Maley, after a slow start at Parkhead he was loaned to Clydebank in 1923. After 13 goals in 30 games, including the winner versus Celtic, he was recalled.

In his second spell, the records tumbled, as he became the top marksman in European football with 49 and 50 league goals respectively in seasons 1926/27 and 1935/36.

McGrory had wonderful nicknames. 'Human Torpedo' and 'The Mermaid', because of his acrobatic heading ability and [illegible]er, even though he was not the tallest at around 5' 6". His prowes[illegible] the air to hover 'hawk-like' and flick the ball as fiercely as most players could kick it ensured a high percentage of his goals were from headers.

Scoring McGrory propelled Celtic to two Scottish League titles and four Scottish Cups at a time when Rangers where the dominant force in Scottish football.

Famously, in the Scottish Cup semi-final of 1925, McGrory scored twice in a historic five-nil win versus the old enemy at Hampden Park, before a record crowd for an Old Firm match of over 101,000. In the final, after a Patsy Gallagher equaliser, McGrory scored a last-minute winner to beat Dundee 2-1.

McGrory scored further cup final winners, in both finals versus Motherwell – in 1931 he hit two in the 4-2 replay triumph after also scoring in the initial 2-2 draw, and in 1933 he scored the only goal of the game in the 55th Scottish Cup Final.

His last Scottish Cup Final appearance was in his farewell full season with Celtic as the Hoops beat Aberdeen 2-1 in April 1937, winning the cup for a 15th time before a British club record crowd at Hampden Park of 146,433, the largest ever attendance for a domestic match in Europe.

A decade had separated his two league titles – 1925/26 and the record breaking 1935/36 season when he scored a club record 50 league goals and for the second time in his career was the leading goalscorer throughout the European leagues.

McGrory's work ethic and instinctive God-given gift enabled him to perform superhuman individual goalscoring feats. On 14th January 1928 he scored eight goals in a single match for Celtic versus Dunfermline Athletic in a 9-0 victory. Reportedly none of his eight goals had come from his head! This remains a record for a top-flight match in British football for an individual player. He also holds the record for most hat-tricks, with 55 throughout his professional playing career.

Even allowing for the fact that there were far fewer internationals at this time, remarkably McGrory was only capped seven times (controversy over the selection policy), he still managed five goals. Most celebrated was his double versus England in April 1933 in a 2-1 victory, with the winner giving rise to the birth of 'The Hampden Roar', such was the jubilation among Scotland followers in a crowd of 134,170.

With knee injuries, McGrory retired from the game, but not before he had in his final competitive match in October 1937 versus Queens Park in a 4-3 win at Parkhead, scored his 408th league goal and 550th in total, including goals in the Glasgow Cup and Charity Cup.

During the Second World War, he worked as a chief storeman at a munitions factory in Ayrshire and also joined the Home Guard.

Entering management, he guided Kilmarnock to the Scottish Cup Final in 1938 and managed Celtic for 20 years from 1945, winning the league in 1953/54, two Scottish Cups in 1951 and 1954 and two Scottish League Cups in 1956/57 and 1957/58, with a record score in an English or Scottish final of 7-1 with victory versus Rangers. He then in 1965 handed over the reins to Jock Stein.

Goalscoring forever, McGrory had personal attributes of fair play, sportsmanship and virtuous religious beliefs of bravery and loyalty. He displayed these often and especially so in the summer of 1928, when he stayed loyal to Celtic when Herbert Chapman's Arsenal wanted to sign him for a world record fee of £10,000, which would have made him the highest paid footballer in Britain.

Content and happy to remain in Glasgow, he commented, "McGrory of Arsenal just never sounded as good as McGrory of Celtic."

Today supporters remember, singing the Celtic anthem, "Tell me the old, old story, a hat-trick for McGrory... he will carry us through."

Vic Watson

Like all players of the era, Vic Watson scored his goals 'off camera'. If you were not in attendance at the match, the only way to see football was through British Pathe/Movietone News – in the cinema playing footage from FA Cup Finals and internationals.

The footballers seemed to move at a similar speed as horseback riders in the early Westerns. During the Roaring 20s and into the 1930s, Vic Watson may not have been a film star but his tremendous goalscoring talent ensured his star quality shone brightly in the colours of West Ham United.

The one occasion Watson did find himself on screen was the first FA Cup Final to take place at the new Empire Stadium, Wembley in April 1923. Second Division West Ham had reached the final versus Bolton Wanderers after beating Derby County 5-2 in the semi-final at Stamford Bridge. West Ham were enjoying their time in the spotlight, having been a non-league side only four years previously.

The 1923 final shall be forever remembered as the 'White Horse Final' as a grey horse called Billy and a police officer with the footballing name PC George Scorey, found themselves at the centre of a record crowd of 126,047 with some estimates of over 200,000 in attendance. The match was delayed for 45 minutes and, unfortunately for Vic and his West Ham teammates, Bolton ran out 2-0 winners.

Watson was a veteran of the First World War and out of service with work hard to find. He played for his home town club Girton and also turned out for Cambridge Town and Wellingborough Town. He travelled to Peterborough to find employment and played for his works engineering football team.

He was signed by West Ham manager Syd King for the best £50 (to my knowledge as a gesture of goodwill, as Watson was an amateur and free agent) the club have ever spent and made his league debut in 1920. The Hammers had only just been elected to the Football League in 1919, having played in the Southern League.

He was initially signed as cover for Sydney Puddefoot, who then moved on, but his goalscoring soon made an impression and his 27 goals in season 1922/23 saw West Ham promoted to the First Division and reach the FA Cup Final, both for the first time in club history.

1923 was also the year Watson gained international honours, winning the first of five England caps, scoring on debut versus Wales in a 2-2 draw at Ninian Park, Cardiff. In total he scored four international goals, including two versus Scotland at Wembley in a 5-2 victory in the 1930 British Home Championship.

In the 1925/26 season, he scored 20 league goals as West Ham finished sixth. During the 1929/30 season, Watson, now in his 33rd year, realised a personal ambition by topping the First Division goalscoring charts with a club record 42 league goals including hat-tricks versus Aston Villa (5-2) and Leeds United (3-0), scoring 50 goals in 44 games in all competitions.

In season 1931/32, he found the net 23 times in the league, but after nine seasons of top-flight football West Ham were relegated. Watson's record in the top flight stands comparison with any goalscorer over an extended period of goalscoring consistency. Over the nine top-flight seasons he scored 203 league goals in 295 appearances for a side that were often battling the drop.

The following season, with Watson scoring 28 league and cup goals, West Ham as a second division club reached their first FA Cup semi-final for ten years. Watson and West Ham found themselves up against Dixie Dean's Everton. He did score in the match at Molineux but Everton and Dixie won through 2-1.

In 1935, Watson left East London. His goalscoring figures for West Ham United are incredible. 326 goals in 505 appearances, 298 league goals in 462 appearances, including six versus Leeds United in an 8-2 First Division match in February 1929 at the Boleyn Ground. It would be some 40 years later before a certain Geoff Hurst equalled Vic's individual club scoring record of a double hat-trick.

Joining Southampton, he scored a further 14 league goals for the Saints, including a hat-trick v Nottingham Forest in February 1936, aged 38 years 3 months.

He returned to his home town of Girton and became a market gardener, where in 1946 he coached Cambridge City to the East Anglian Cup. He was among the guests of honour when Cambridge City opened their floodlights against West Ham in February 1959.

In 2010, a commemorative plaque was unveiled in his place of birth. Victor 'Vic' Watson ex-West Ham & England 'Record Goalscorer'. Born and died in Girton.

Vic is one of only eleven players in the history of English football with 300 or more league goals.

1950s & 1960s

As league football resumed, supporters flocked to stadiums up and down the country, establishing record attendances in the late 1940s and early 1950s. With the newly renamed and adapted Division 3 and Division 4, from 1951 the Football League membership became the 92 clubs.

Many players had their football careers interrupted, shortened, delayed and in some cases ended by the second of the World Wars. Men such as Albert Stubbins, who was prolific during wartime for Newcastle United and won the first post-war league title with Liverpool and was the only footballer to appear on the The Beatles' iconic album cover, *Sgt. Pepper's Lonely Hearts Club Band* (rubbing shoulders with Laurel & Hardy and Marlene Dietrich).

This period saw the expansion of international football competition, which would ultimately see English football's greatest triumph in 1966, the introduction of European club football from 1955 and the Football League Cup from 1960. Goalscorers at all levels were now testing themselves against new opponents and defensive formations.

Goalscorers of the time included:

Bristol frontmen John Ayteo in the red of City, with 315 league goals and in the blue and white quarters of Rovers, Geoff Bradford was also creating club records with 245 in the league.

In the 1960/61 season, Terry Bly scored a post-war individual record of 52 league goals as Peterborough United won the Fourth Division Championship with a league record of 134 league goals.

One club servant for Luton Town, Gordon Turner, scored 243 league goals for the Hatters, including the season they were promoted to Division 1 for the first time in 1955 after some 70 years since being formed in 1885.

The goalscoring partnership of Tony Richards and Colin Taylor together at Walsall in the 50s and 60s amazingly ended with a club record 184 league goals each.

For a decade Sammy Collins at Torquay United: 204 league goals.

Wilf Mannion, 'the Golden Boy' of Middlesbrough FC and part of the 'famous five' England forward line.

Joe Baker scored over 100 goals in both England and Scotland and was among the first British footballers to play abroad, with Torino in Italy.

Ivor Allchurch 'the Golden Boy of Welsh Football': 166 league goals in two spells with Swansea City and at one time a record 23 international goals for Wales, including scoring twice at the 1958 World Cup.

Craggy Scot Tommy Johnston was the top scorer for Orient both in a season and on aggregate. Tony Hateley, father of Mark, scored over 200 league goals, mainly for Notts County.

Jeff Astle scored a FA Cup Final winner for West Brom and was also First Division top scorer.

Neil Martin: 200 plus league goals for eight clubs, with over 100 league goals in both the Scottish and English leagues.

Cliff Holton, reported to have one of the fiercest shots in post-war football, started as a full back and wing back, and went onto bag 295 league goals.

Busby Babe Dennis Violett: record top scorer for Manchester United in a single league season and scorer of the club's first goal in European competition.

Len Shackleton, the 'Clown Prince of Soccer', with over 100 goals for Sunderland.

Scottish international Alan Gilzean: over 150 goals for Dundee and over 100 for Tottenham Hotspur.

John O'Rourke with 164 league goals, particularly prolific with Luton Town, Middlesbrough and Ipswich Town.

Ron Saunders: over 200 league goals, mostly for Portsmouth, probably best known for managing Aston Villa to the League Championship in 1980/81.

Keith Wagstaff: 'Waggy' scored over 300 league and cup goals with Mansfield Town and Hull City, many in partnership with Chris Chilton.

Charlie Wayman: 5 league clubs, 255 league goals with over 100 for Preston North End.

Dennis Westcott: 124 goals in 144 games for the Wolves, including 38 league goals as First Division top scorer in 1946/47. Also prolific for Blackburn Rovers, Manchester City and Chesterfield.

In the Irish League, Jimmy Jones scored over 600 goals in all competitions.

John Charles

'Il Buon Gigante', The Gentle Giant.

John Charles is held in the highest esteem for his professionalism and fair play on the football pitch, having never been booked or sent off in his playing career as a centre-half and centre-forward and for generosity off the pitch at charity events, giving away all his Welsh international caps at fundraisers.

Son Mel, said, "He would do anything for anybody, and we grew up knowing this."

His versatility and character is deserving of adulation. Former England manager Bobby Robson said Charles was the only footballer who was world class in two positions. England forward Nat Lofthouse named Charles as the best defender he ever faced, while England centre-half and his country's first centurion, Billy Wright, said he was the best forward he had ever come up against.

British football's greatest ever export, he was the first foreign player to be inducted into the Italian Football Hall of Fame ahead of Michel Platini and Diego Maradona. In 2001, when he returned on a visit to Juventus, while walking round the running track of the Stadio delle Alpi he received a wonderful reception with the entire crowd chanting his name. In his autobiography, *King John*, Charles said, "I was stunned, I have to admit it brought a tear to my eye."

John Charles was equally adored by fans of Leeds United, with a stand at Elland Road named in his honour and he is acclaimed as the most influential Welsh footballer of all time.

Such a legacy was achieved through a natural footballing ability with a modest, unassuming personality; a footballing all-rounder able to play at both ends of the pitch, but with his goals record in England and Italy, by definition a goalscorer.

After the war, he joined home town club Swansea Town on the ground staff and even as a teenager he was a force to be reckoned with, 6' 2", marvellous physique, strong, talented, fast, good in the air with two good feet and great ball control.

He was spotted by Leeds' Welsh scout Jack Pickard and along with brother Mel went for a trial with the Second Division club, then managed by Major Frank Buckley.

After playing in various positions across the back line for the reserves, he made his league debut aged 17 in April 1949 at centre-half. When he was given a run of games up front, he impressed and by 1952/53 he had enjoyed his first full season at centre-forward, scoring 26 goals.

The following season he was the football league's leading goalscorer with 42 league goals, with Leeds finishing 10th in Division 2.

In 1955/56 his 29 goals saw Leeds promoted back to the top flight. In his first season at the highest level, he was the First Division top scorer for 1956/57 with 38 of Leeds' 76 league goals. His tally is the second most goals scored in a top-flight season since the Second World War and included hat-tricks in both Yorkshire derbies versus Sheffield Wednesday.

John Charles was now a superstar, but he remained quiet and humble. That same season, Leeds United's West Stand burnt down and the cost of rebuilding for a club already in debt forced Leeds to sell their most prized asset.

Charles joined Juventus in August 1957 for a world record fee of £65,000. In his debut season, 1957/58, he was the top scorer in Serie A with 28 league goals. He is the one player to be the leading scorer in both the English and Italian top flights.

In five seasons with the 'Old Lady' of Italian football he was a revelation, scoring 93 goals in 155 Serie A appearances, winning three Scudettos in 1957/58, 1959/60 and 1960/61 and two Coppa Italia, scoring in both finals versus Inter in 1959 and Fiorentina in 1960. His performances saw him twice named Footballer of the Year, without a single caution to his name, earning him film star status across Italy.

Charles returned to Leeds in 1962 where in total he completed 327 appearances with 157 goals including 11 hat-tricks. He left for Italy again to Roma for £70,000, but his best years where behind him and he later admitted that he had left Juve too soon.

His career ended with spells at Cardiff City and as player/manager of non-league Hereford United and he also turned out for Merthyr Tydfil.

For Wales, John Charles won 38 international caps, scoring 15 times. He would have won many more caps but was not always released by Juventus for international duty. He helped his country qualify for their first World Cup finals in 1958, scoring in the 1-1 draw with Hungary and reach the quarter-finals, but unfortunately injury kept him out of the match versus Brazil and a young Pele. He also represented Great Britain versus Europe in 1955.

His reputation and playing deeds are best summed up by a tribute from Leeds United and England World Cup winner Jack Charlton: "The most effective player I ever saw, the one that made the most difference to the performance of the whole team, was without question, John Charles."

Brian Clough

In a previous life, before Cloughie the managerial motivator, a young man called Brian was a most prolific goalscorer.

251 football league goals in 274 football league appearances at a strike rate of 91.61. Data comparable with one of sport's most distinctive

records, the 99.94 Test Match batting average of iconic Australian cricketer Donald Bradman. B.C Before Cloughie, A.D After Don.

Brian Clough completed the quickest 200 football league goals in September 1961 after only 219 league appearances. It's not as if he slowed down after reaching his double century, scoring another 51 in 55 appearances before a career-ending injury, playing for Sunderland at Roker Park versus Bury, aged 27, on Boxing Day 1962.

He tried in vain over the next two years to recover (playing a few games) but his football playing career was at an end.

As a teenager he was spotted by Middlesbrough scout and record goalscorer George Camsell and signed in 1952. "I've got to thank George obviously for getting me to Middlesbrough." With Clough on National Service with the RAF, he had to wait to establish himself with the first team, making his debut for his home town club in 1955.

With Boro he scored 197 league goals in 213 league appearances, 204 goals in 222 games in all competitions – a goal a game record. With a post-war record of 121 league goals over seasons 1957/58 (40 goals), 1958/59 (42 goals) and 1959/60 (39 goals), Clough was the first player to be leading goalscorer in a single division (Second Division) for three consecutive seasons.

In season 1958/59, with 42 league goals he was the top scorer in the Football League, all the more incredible as Middlesbrough ended the season in 13th place. On the opening day of the season in August 1958 he scored five in a club record 9-0 win over newly promoted Brighton. In the return fixture at the Goldstone Ground in December there were ten goals, with Cloughie bagging a hat-trick in a 6-4 away win.

In October 1960, he was involved in an even more historic match, helping himself to a hat-trick. Score line: Charlton Athletic 6-6 Middlesbrough, one of only two such high scoring draws in English league competition. The other occasion being 30 years earlier when another ace goalscorer, David Halliday, also bagged a hat-trick.

At representative level he also showed his worth, scoring all five goals for the Football League versus the Irish League at Windsor Park, Belfast in September 1959. The following month he won his only two England caps, playing up front with Jimmy Greaves versus Wales at Ninian Park, Cardiff and versus Sweden at Wembley Stadium.

Never one to hide his feelings, Clough expressed his disappointment at not being selected more often for his country at international level. He also made public accusations that his Boro team mates were betting against their own side and deliberately conceding goals. Despite his extraordinary goalscoring consistency on Teesside, the club never gained promotion to the top flight.

In the summer of 1961, he moved to Sunderland for a club record fee of £48,000. In his first season, 1961/62, he scored 29 league goals in 34 appearances, including a hat-trick in a 7-2 victory against Swansea Town. On Wearside he scored 54 league goals in 61 league appearances, the fateful injury bringing his playing days to a premature end. In 1965 he had a testimonial match, scoring twice for Sunderland v Newcastle United.

Staying on in his native North East he began his managerial career that same year, with Hartlepool, the youngest manager in the Football League, aged 30. He would go on to manage Derby County, Brighton, Leeds United (for 44 days) and Nottingham Forest, usually assisted by his former Boro team mate and close friend Peter Taylor.

One of the first 'tracksuit managers' before his trademark green jumper, Clough achieved legendary status leading Derby to promotion and the First Division Championship in 1971/72. He repeated the success at Forest, winning the title again in 1977/78, plus four League Cups and immortality with two European Cups in 1979 and 1980. At Forest he also managed his son Nigel. When he retired as manager of Nottingham Forest at the end of the 1992/93 season, he received an emotional and heartfelt farewell in his final home match at the City Ground for all the glory and pride he had brought to the club.

The A52 between both cities is known as the Brian Clough Way and he has statues in his honour in Middlesbrough, Derby and Nottingham. He also has a stand named in his honour at the City Ground. Derby and Forest compete for the Brian Clough Trophy when they meet in any given league season.

Everyone it seems was aware of Old Big 'Ead, a smiling Muhammad Ali looking straight at the camera on television, said, "I'm the talker... now Clough, I've had enough" referring to Brian's reputation for his ability to express himself.

In 2017, UEFA named Cloughie among their Top 10 coaches. Not quite in the 'Top One' as he once claimed, though arguably he was as a goalscorer.

Ray Crawford

Nicknamed 'Jungle Boy' by the football writers after 18 months National Service guarding plantations in Malaya (now Malaysia), Ray Crawford called his autobiography *Curse of the Jungle Boy*.

"The curse was this," he explained. "I left Portsmouth, they got relegated, I left Ipswich, they got relegated, I left Wolves, they got relegated. At West Brom, I played in the semi-final of the League Cup, scored the goals to get them to the final, left the next day to go back to Ipswich, and Albion lost the final to QPR, who were in Division Three."

Every time he left a club, something went wrong. However, as a goalscorer he was blessed! Having put down his rifle, he would become one of the deadliest marksmen of his generation. 289 League goals in 476 appearances for seven clubs across the leagues.

Just turned 21, he began his Football League career with hometown club Portsmouth in August 1957. The following August, after 9 league goals in 19 appearances, he moved to Ipswich Town, then managed by Alf Ramsey.

In two spells, Crawford became the club's record goalscorer – a penalty box footballer, great header of a ball, as he spearheaded the attack in partnership with Ted Phillips at Portman Road, beginning the most successful period in the history of Ipswich Town Football Club.

In season 1960/61, he was the Second Division top scorer with 39 league goals, including a hat-trick versus Leeds (5-2) and goals in both East Anglian derbies versus Norwich, as Ipswich won the divisional championship with a club record 100 goals.

The following season, 1961/62, Ipswich Town made history, with Crawford as the First Division top scorer (shared with Derek Kevan, WBA) with 33 league goals, including a hat-trick versus Chelsea (5-2), as Town were crowned Champions of England for the first time. It was also the first time a club won the First Division title in their first season in the top flight.

Two goals by Crawford on the final day of the season in a 2-0 win over Aston Villa at Portman Road clinched the league ahead of the two previous seasons' champions, Burnley and Spurs, with Ray finding the net against both clubs during the season. Ipswich's achievement is all the more remarkable, considering as recently as season 1956/57 they were in Division 3 (South).

Now the best team in the land and with the country's most prolific goalscorer, Crawford was rewarded with international recognition, winning his two England caps during the title winning season of 1961/62, both at Wembley – a debut versus Northern Ireland and scoring in a 3-1 victory over Austria.

In 1962/63, Ipswich had their first campaign in Europe. Crawford became the first British player to score five goals in a single European match as Ipswich run up a club record 10-0 victory over Floriana (Malta). He actually scored seven goals over the two legs in a 14-1 aggregate victory.

In the next round, he famously scored in a second leg 2-1 success at Portman Road over AC Milan as Ipswich exited the European Cup 4-2 on aggregate to the season's eventual winners.

Crawford moved around, having spells in the Midlands with Wolves (39 league goals in 57 appearances) and WBA (6 league goals in 14 appearances), before returning to Ipswich the year Alf won the World Cup with England.

His goals again returned Ipswich to the top flight as Second Division Champions in the 1967/68 season. In his two spells with the Suffolk club (1958-63 and 1966-69) Ray Crawford scored a club record 203 league goals in 320 appearances, with 228 goals in total.

He achieved the unique double of being top scorer in the Second Division and First Division with championship winning sides in successive seasons. He was considered the Pride of East Anglia.

He also played for Charlton Athletic (7 league goals in 21 appearances), then for non-league Kettering Town. In August 1970, he was back in the football league, signed by Dick Graham, manager of Fourth Division Colchester United where he would score 25 goals in 45 league appearances, with arguably the most famous goals coming in the twilight of his career in the FA cup giant killing of Leeds United in the 5th Round in 1971, scoring twice in a 3-2 win.

He also played in South Africa (where he challenged apartheid) before he returned to Pompey as a coach and regular supporter, collecting football autographs in his book for charity auctions.

"Football excited me, and it still excites me now, seeing wingers take people on and strikers scoring great goals."

Ray Crawford's transfer fees were barely more than £100,000 and at his peak with Ipswich he was on £25 to £30 a week, but his goals were priceless, over 300 of them, courtesy of a blessed top scorer league champion.

Ron Davies

Described as the finest centre-forward in Europe by Manchester United manager Matt Busby, Davies scored all four Southampton goals in a famous victory for the Saints at Old Trafford in August 1969.

King Ron certainly was the most prolific target man around. The first post-war footballer to be the league's leading scorer in consecutive seasons. His goalscoring record is all the more astounding as he generally found himself playing for clubs struggling at the wrong end of the table and he still managed to outscore all his contemporaries.

Born in Holywell, Northeast Wales, Davies signed his first professional contract over the border with Fourth Division Chester, aged 17, in the summer of 1959, making his debut the following year in the spring of 1960.

Chester encouraged the strapping teenager to leap hurdles in army boots to develop his jumping ability as a powerful header of the ball. Years later he recalled, “When I took those boots off, I felt I could jump over the moon, but I was told it would catch up with me.” It certainly did the trick as far as goalscoring was concerned.

Davies struck 44 league goals in 94 appearances for a Chester side that flirted with re-election to the Football League, finishing in 91st and 92nd place.

In season 1962/63 he moved onto Luton Town, but not even his goals (21 in 32 league appearances), which included all four in a 4-2 win versus Norwich City, could save the Hatters from relegation to the Third Division.

The following season, he was on the move again for a club record transfer fee of £30,000 to Norwich. Over three seasons in the Second Division at Carrow Road he kept up his goal average with 58 in the league from 113 appearances.

Much to the annoyance of Canary fans, the Norwich board sold Ron to Southampton in 1966 for another club record fee of £55,000.

Newly promoted to the First Division for the first time in club history, Davies, aged 24, would also have his first opportunity of top-flight English football.

Developing a lethal partnership with Martin Chivers, in his first three seasons at the Dell he scored 85 league goals in 119 appearances. Goalscoring figures at the highest level that only Dixie Dean and Jimmy Greaves could live with.

In 1966/67, he was the First Division and football league top scorer with 37 of Southampton’s total of 74, including four versus Aston Villa in a 6-2 win (43 goals in all competitions), all as the Saints just avoided relegation in 19th place. In a time before all goals were on television, only one of his league tally of 37 was recorded by the cameras, on *Match of the Day*, Leeds United 0 Southampton 1 in October 1966.

In 1967/68, he was top scorer again with 28 league goals, shared with George Best and another four-goal haul, this time away to Chelsea, 6-2.

In 1968/69, Davies hit another 20 league goals as Southampton finished in a club high position of 7th in the league and qualified for Europe, where he top scored with four. including scoring the Saints’ first goal in European football in the first round second leg match versus Rosenborg, a 2-0 victory in the Fairs Cup at The Dell in October 1969.

During seven magnificent goalscoring seasons with the Saints, his record reads: 134 league goals in 240 appearances. 153 goals in all competitions in 281 games. Southampton team mate Mick Channon said, "He could head a ball harder than I could kick it, nobody ever came close to Ron Davies in that department."

He moved along the South Coast to Portsmouth, scoring 18 league goals in 59 appearances and in November 1974 he was signed by Manchester United, who had been relegated the previous season, but Davies was only played 8 times, all from the bench. In the Third Division with Millwall, he ended his football league career with a further three appearances. In total: 275 league goals from 549 league appearances.

As an international, he represented Wales 29 times, scoring 9 goals. He scored on his debut in 1964 versus Northern Ireland. In the 1968/69 Home Internationals he scored versus England at Wembley and twice against Scotland.

On the recommendation of Bestie, Ron joined George in the North American Soccer League (NASL) with the LA Aztecs. His goals helped the club to the play-offs in 1976 and 1977 and he also played for the Tulsa Roughnecks and Seattle Sounders.

Davies settled in the States where he coached at various levels. His interests also included fishing and he was a talented artist with published cartoon and caricatures of his team mates.

As it was, Ron's training regime as a teenager did catch up with him when he needed hip replacements. To help pay for his American medical expenses Southampton fans organised a 'Give it to Ron Appeal' holding a 'Ron Davies Day' to raise funds. Supporters of his former clubs, including Chester and Norwich, also contributed, as did the Welsh FA, BBC and ITV.

Ron had always said, "Fans do not receive the credit they deserve, that without fans, football is nothing."

Supporters had certainly not forgotten, especially those of Southampton FC, who had chanted in his heyday, "His name is Ronnie Davies, he's the leader of the team."

Jimmy Greaves

The greatest goalscorer of all-time in the history of English football.

Aged 31, Jimmy Greaves retired from the game 50 years ago after a playing career of goalscoring excellence at the highest level.

Only in the last few seasons have modern day all-time greats Cristiano Ronaldo and Lionel Messi caught up with Greavsie's top-flight record of 366 league goals (one ahead of Gerd 'Der Bomber' Muller) in the major European Leagues.

A carefree personality combined with a natural born gift for goalscoring. It was ever thus, at schoolboy level he used to predict how many goals he would score.

Signed by Chelsea, Greaves scored 114 goals in one year for the youth team. Aged 17, he made his league debut for the Blues, scoring versus Tottenham Hotspur at White Hart Lane in August 1957. On Christmas Day 1957, he scored four in a 7-4 victory over Portsmouth, creating a record as the youngest goalscorer of a top-flight hat-trick in English football history, aged 17 years 10 months.

In four seasons at Stamford Bridge, he totalled 124 league goals in 157 appearances, 132 goals in 169 games in all competitions.

Although playing for a mid-table side, he was the First Division top scorer in 1958/59 with 32 goals including five versus Wolves (6-2) and 1960/61 with 41 goals, a post-war top-flight record which also included a record six hat-tricks. Greaves also played for a London representative team and scored in the original European Fairs Cup Final in 1958 versus Barcelona. In the 1959/60 season, he again hit five in the league, away at Preston North End in a nine-goal thriller, 5-4 to the Blues.

On 19th November 1960, versus Manchester City, aged 20 years 9 months with a hat-trick in a 6-3 win, he became the youngest player to complete a century of football league goals. A few weeks later he notched his third five-goal haul in the league, in a 7-1 victory over West Bromwich Albion at the Bridge.

Motivated by a desire for on-field success and extra money, he put in a transfer request. On his final appearance for Chelsea in April 1961, he was made captain and scored all his side's four goals versus Nottingham Forest.

He moved to AC Milan in the summer of 1961, ironically just as the maximum wage was abolished in English football. Disillusioned by the football and restricted lifestyle in Italy he sought a way back home. In December 1961, Spurs' double winning manager Bill Nicholson signed Greaves, famously for £99,999. In Serie A he scored 9 goals in 10 appearances, qualifying for a championship winners medal, as Milan went on to win the league.

Bill Nic said, "I wanted to him sign from the moment I saw him score his first goal in league football on his Chelsea debut at White Hart Lane. What a tremendous goal it was! He beat three defenders before stroking the ball in the back of the net. It had all the hallmarks of his game – improvisation and genius."

Greavsie hit a hat-trick on his Spurs league debut versus Blackpool and by the end of the season had helped the club retain the FA Cup, scoring nine goals in the cup run including a goal in the semi-final versus Manchester United (3-1) and the opening goal in the 3-1 final victory over Burnley.

In the 1962/63 season he scored twice in the final of the European Cup Winners' Cup versus Atletico Madrid in Rotterdam on 15th May 1963 as Spurs won 5-1 to become the first British team to win a European club trophy.

In the league and cup he recorded a personal best of 44 goals for a season, 37 in the league, making him First Division top scorer with Spurs runners-up, and overall leading league goalscorer, five in Europe and two in the 5-1 Charity Shield win over Ipswich Town. Greaves's league tally included four-goal hauls versus Nottingham Forest (9-2), Liverpool (7-2) and a hat-trick versus Manchester United (6-2).

This would be the first of three consecutive seasons as the top flight's highest goalscorer, with 35 and 29 league goals respectively in 1963/64 and 1964/65 (shared with Andy McEvoy, Blackburn Rovers), the first time in the history of English football a player had achieved this feat. During the 1964/65 season in September 1964, Jimmy also scored both of Spurs' first goals on the new *Match of the Day* recorded highlights football programme in a 3-2 defeat at West Ham United.

Nothing it seemed could stop Greavsie's goalscoring... In eight successive top-flight seasons from 1957/58 to 1964/65 he scored 20 plus league goals, but in 1965/66 he was out of football for three months, having contracted hepatitis, admitting it had taken a yard off his pace. Returning to the Spurs first team, he was included in the England squad for the World Cup. Playing in the first three group games he was then forced to miss the quarter-final with Argentina due to injury. Recovered for the semi-final, Alf Ramsey continued with replacement Geoff Hurst and Roger Hunt up front. With no substitutions, Greaves did not play in the final, enduring the biggest disappointment of his football career.

His international records reads 44 goals, 57 caps. As always, he scored on debut, versus Peru in Lima in May 1959, on England's tour of the Americas. He scored for England versus Argentina at the 1962 World Cup in Chile and in 1963 past Lev Yashin in a 2-1 England win over the Rest of the World side at Wembley. Greavsie holds the record for most England international hat-tricks with six including a treble in the record 9-3 game versus Scotland at Wembley in April 1961. Denis Law remembers: "That day, Jimmy Greaves was, as ever, lethal. He was the best pure striker, the best goalscorer, I have ever seen. I didn't want Greaves playing for the opposing team at any time. That's how good he was."

In 1966/67 Spurs won the first all London 'Cockney Cup final' versus his old club Chelsea. Greavsie scored in the semi-final versus Forest, though for once did not find the net in the final. Throughout his career he scored 35 FA Cup goals.

In 1968/69 he was the league and First Division top goalscorer with 27 goals – for an unprecedented sixth time the leading top-flight goalscorer, overtaking Steve Bloomer's record of five. Jimmy's total included four in a 5-1 Spurs win over Sunderland at White Hart Lane.

This would prove to be Greavsie's final full season with Spurs, a glorious goalscoring love affair between player and club: 220 league goals in 321 appearances, 266 in all competitions in 379 games, both club goalscoring records (including Charity Shield, 268 in 381).

In March 1970 in an exchange deal involving Martin Peters, he moved to West Ham, playing up front with Geoff Hurst. Once again Greavsie scored on debut (as he had done so for Chelsea, England, Milan and Spurs), twice in a 5-1 away league win at Manchester City.

Hurst said, "You hear the term 'Genius' and it is the one word which applies to Jimmy… You are talking about the greatest goalscorer we have ever seen." After both their playing days were over, Geoff and Jimmy would go on theatre tours together.

As the 1969/70 club season ended with Jimmy knowing he would not be part of the England squad for the Mexico World Cup, he did what seemed the most logical alternative, entering the London to Mexico World Cup Rally! A 16,000-mile drive from Wembley through Europe and South America ending in Mexico City's Aztec Stadium. Hired by Ford (he lived close to their Dagenham factory) alongside rally driver Tony Fall in a black and white Escort No. 26, Jimmy and Tony completed the race, finishing in a very creditable 6th place.

Upon reaching Mexico City, Greavsie, found a way into the British

Embassy to look up his old friend and team mate Bobby Moore (involved in a jewellery incident), jokingly asking Mooro, "Where he'd hidden the bracelet."

After Greavsie's escapades he had one more season in league football with West Ham, in total 13 league goals in 38 appearances.

He retired from league football aged 31 at the end of the 1970/71 season, which included a goal at White Hart Lane in a 2-2 draw, and still, 50 years on, is the holder of the two most prized records in football, 357 top-flight English league goals and six times top-flight leading scorer. In total Greaves has 422 goals in club football.

He returned to football after a four-year absence at non-league level with Brentwood, Chelmsford City, Barnet and Woodford Town.

He documented his personal drinking problems in his autobiography *This One's on Me* and the subsequent frank and honest television documentary *Just for Today*, based on the book.

After stints as part of the 1982 World Cup panel, ITV teamed Jimmy up with Ian St. John for the hugely popular award-winning *Saint and Greavsie,* which ran from 1985 to 1992 on Saturday lunchtimes. 'It's a funny old game.'

In February 2020, the month of Greavsie 80th birthday, the *Daily Mail* launched a 'Gong for Greavsie' campaign with support from Geoff Hurst, José Mourinho and Harry Kane.

He was subsequently awarded an MBE. Thousands had signed a petition of support online, signatures that doubtless included the privileged to have seen Jimmy Greaves play, and for the rest of us an acknowledgement to the greatest goalscorer in the history of English football, highlighted in the wonderful *BT Sport* film *Greavsie.*

On Sunday 19th September 2021, our greatest ever goalscorer quietly passed away. RIP James Peter Greaves, 'Jim'.

David Herd

In 1950, a year after the LS Lowry football painting *The Football Match*, David Herd signed for Stockport County. Twenty years later, he hung up his boots in 1970, the same year George Harrison released *All Things Must Pass*, a goalscoring career that spanned 20 seasons throughout the cultural sea changes of the 1950s and 1960s. He scored 269 club goals, including 222 in the First Division, placing Herd 5th on the post-war list of leading top-flight goalscorers and 15th on the all-time list in the history of English league football.

On 5th May 1951 at Edgeley Park, something that is probably unique in English football league history occurred, the first known father and son duo in league football, as David played alongside his father Alec in the forward line for Stockport versus Hartlepool in the Third Division (North), David marking the occasion by scoring in a 2-0 home win.

His father Alec had won the FA Cup in 1934 with Manchester City, just a few weeks before son David was born in Hamilton, Lanarkshire, being brought up in Moss Side, Manchester.

By the end of the 1951/52 season, he had 6 league goals in 16 appearances for Stockport in the Third Division (North). In the summer of 1952, he was called up for his National Service. After being demobbed from the RAF, he was signed in August 1954 by Arsenal for £10,000, making his debut in February 1955, two months before his 21st birthday.

In seven seasons at Highbury, he scored 97 League goals in 166 appearances, with 107 goals in all competitions, and was nicknamed 'Hotshot Herd' because of his explosive right foot shooting power.

He scored in the historic 4-5 home defeat to Manchester United on 1st February 1958, which proved to be the 'Busby Babes' last match on English soil, coming five days before the Munich Air Disaster.

Despite all his goals, Arsenal's highest league finish during his time at the club was 3rd in season 1958/59. Herd himself was the second highest scorer in the First Division in season 1960/61 with 29 league goals, including hat-tricks versus Newcastle United (5-0) and Manchester City (5-4).

In the summer of 1961, he was on his way to Old Trafford, with United paying the Gunners £40,000 for his goalscoring services. Again, like at Arsenal, he would play for seven seasons, scoring on his United debut in the FA Cup, League Cup and all three European competitions.

In his second season (1962/63), having just avoided relegation, Man Utd reached the FA Cup Final, which had been delayed for three weeks because of a backlog of fixtures through the winter 'big freeze'. David was the difference, scoring twice past Gordon Banks. For the first time since 1948, the Red Devils had won the cup, beating Leicester City 3-1 and David had emulated his dad as an FA Cup winner.

In season 1964/65 Herd was a league champion as United won the closest of title races on goal average from Leeds United, highlights included a David Herd double in the 4-0 defeat of Chelsea. In 1965/66 he scored a career best 33 goals with 24 in the league, including hat-tricks against Fulham (4-1) and Burnley (4-2).

Another league championship followed in 1966/67 during which, in November 1966, Herd scored a unique hat-trick (four goals in total) against three separate goalkeepers versus Sunderland. A month later in December, he scored a hat-trick in a United 4-3 away win at West Brom.

Herd enjoyed playing in Europe, with 14 goals, including a double versus Spurs in the Old Trafford second leg 4-1 victory, 4-3 on aggregate in the Battle of the English giants in the 1963/64 Cup Winners' Cup. He helped United to reach two European semi-finals in the Fairs Cup in 1964/65 and the European Cup in 1965/66, but unfortunately a broken leg would deny him playing beyond the quarter-final stage of the 1967/68 campaign, ultimately seeing the club become the first English side to win the European Cup. The pain of injury and disappointment was somewhat eased as Herd was awarded a winner's medal.

His United career was now at an end – 114 league goals in 202 appearances, 145 goals in all competitions.

In the summer of 1968, he was transferred to Stoke City, scoring 11 league goals in 44 appearances for the Victoria Ground club. He also played for Waterford in Ireland and went on to manage Lincoln City.

At international level he was capped five times by Scotland between 1958 and 1961, scoring three goals. He made his debut versus Wales in 1958. His goals at Hampden Park were against Northern Ireland (2-2) and a brace versus the Republic of Ireland in a 4-1 victory.

In his second successful career, he was David Herd, the well-known businessman/garage owner in his adopted home town of Manchester. He is remembered fondly, a player who at his peak had even outscored Best, Law and Charlton. A tough, durable goalscorer from the end of ration book days to the start of colour television – significantly the only player with over 100 goals for both Arsenal and Manchester United.

Roger Hunt

In April 1972, a record attendance of 56,214 for a testimonial match in England gathered to pay homage to a darling of the Kop. As was his wont, Roger Hunt obliged by scoring a hat-trick in an 8-6 victory.

The Anfield faithful knew the value of their 'Blond Bomber'. Eleven seasons of goalscoring craft, graft and sheer hard-running determination had yielded 285 goals for Liverpool FC in 492 appearances, including a club record 244 goals in the league.

After his National Service, Hunt played for Devizes Town, and Stockton Heath in the Mid-Cheshire League where he was spotted by ex-player and Liverpool scout Bill Jones. In the summer of 1958, he was signed as an amateur and on professional terms in July 1959 by manager Phil Taylor.

After impressing in the reserves, he made his Liverpool debut in September 1959, scoring at Anfield versus Scunthorpe. Manager Taylor then resigned and Bill Shankly was appointed in December 1959.

Shanks admired the never say die attitude of Roger and in their second full season together the 1961/62 Second Division Championship was won, with Hunt overall league top scorer with a club record 41 league goals. Over the next three seasons the goals flowed and the glory followed.

In 1963/64 Hunt scored 31 league goals as Liverpool won the league for the time since the Liddell and Stubbins side of 1946/47. Among the 31 were four versus Stoke City on Boxing Day 1963.

In August 1964 Hunt scored the first goal on the new football highlights programme *Match of the Day* when the BBC cameras visited 'Beatleville' as Arsenal were beaten 3-2.

The following month he scored twice in the club's first match in Europe, a 5-0 away win in Iceland versus RK Reykjavik in the European Cup. In November he also scored in the match where, for the first time, Liverpool wore their new 'all red' strip in a 3-0 home victory over Anderlecht.

By the spring the Reds were in the semi-finals of both the FA Cup and the European Cup. After victory over Chelsea at Villa Park in the FA Cup, they faced Leeds United at Wembley, where the ever-reliable Roger Hunt broke the deadlock in extra-time with Ian St. John adding a second to win the cup for the first time in Liverpool's history. "Ee-Ay-Addio, we've won the Cup!" Before the semi-final 1st leg in the European Cup versus World Club Champions Inter Milan, the cup was paraded around Anfield. Hunt again opened the scoring in a 3-1 win, but dubious refereeing decisions in the 2nd leg in Italy saw the Reds eliminated from Europe. In all competitions that season Hunt scored 37 goals.

By 1965/66, Roger was now the foremost forward in English football, he was leading goalscorer in the First Division with 29 league goals, with hat-tricks versus West Ham at Upton Park (5-1), Sunderland (4-0) and a couple versus Everton in the Merseyside derby (5-0) as

Liverpool regained the League Championship.

His goals also saw the club through to their first European Final, where again in a decider he scored, this time in defeat at Hampden Park to Borussia Dortmund in the European Cup Winners' Cup.

In the summer of 1966, he was a World Cup winner with England. Wearing the number 18 shirt, he played in all six matches, scoring three goals, including versus Mexico (2-0) and twice versus France (2-0) on his 28th birthday. He was capped 34 times by his country with 18 international goals, including one on his debut in April 1962 versus Austria (3-1), only twice being on the losing side.

After overtaking Gordon Hodgson's club goalscoring record, Hunt was among the players nearing the end of their time at Anfield as Shanks dismantled an ageing team. Anfield Iron team-mate Tommy Smith said, "Roger Hunt was the best goalscorer I ever saw, he used to create his own goals."

In December 1969 he moved to Bolton Wanderers, signed by his boyhood hero, Nat Lofthouse, adding 24 league goals in 76 appearances. There was also a loan spell with Hellenic in South Africa.

After playing, Hunt was a member of the football pools panel and ran the family haulage business in Culcheth near Warrington.

After his heroics for club and country, Hunt was christened 'Sir Roger' by the Kop, who in the 2020s continue to wave a Roger Hunt flag on match days at Anfield in appreciation of the club's leading league goalscorer of all time.

Please note: Since 2015, it is now known that Roger Hunt scored 244 league goals for Liverpool FC and not 245, which had been the recognised total. The goal that has been 'lost' to Roger's tally was actually an own goal from the Reds match versus Spurs at Anfield in the 1965/66 season. Roger was originally the top scorer in the First Division that season with 30 league goals, now it is 29. However, he remains the leading scorer, shared with Burnley and Northern Ireland international Willie Irvine who also scored 29. The match that Roger overtook Liverpool's leading aggregate league scorer, Gordon Hodgson, is also therefore adjusted. His overall league tally with Liverpool and Bolton is also changed from 269 to 268. Hunt's overall goals total for Liverpool FC in all competitions is now updated from 286 to 285. League 244, FA Cup 18, League Cup 5, Charity Shield 1, Europe 17. And the Kop still chant, "Sir Roger Hunt is wonderful!"

Postscript: Monday 27th September 2021. RIP Roger Hunt. YNWA.

Geoff Hurst

In the summer of 1966 and all that, England and the West Indies played out an iconic Test Cricket series. If things had turned out differently Geoffrey Charles Hurst may well have been lining up against Garfield Sobers

Hurst was a more than capable wicket keeper, representing Essex at first-class level in the County Championship. As it was, Captain Sobers led the tourists to a series victory and Geoff Hurst created his own sporting immortality on a glorious sunny afternoon at Wembley

Stadium on Saturday 30th July.

One swallow does not always make a summer, but this one certainly did. As time goes by the individual achievement accomplished 55 years ago by Geoff Hurst remains omnipresent and is still the one occasion when a footballer has scored a hat-trick in a World Cup Final.

It was only five months earlier, in February 1966, that he had made his international debut versus West Germany in a friendly at Wembley and with a handful of caps was included in Alf Ramsey's World Cup squad.

Hurst did not play in the three group games, but after an injury to Jimmy Greaves he was partnered up front with Roger Hunt, making an instant impression, scoring the only goal of the game in a bad-tempered quarter-final against an ill-disciplined Argentina side. Manager Ramsey was adamant that his players should not swap shirts at the end of the match. Hurst kept his place for the semi-final victory over Portugal and four days later wrote himself into the footballing record books.

In the red of England, in his 8th international appearance, his historic hat-trick of goals past German keeper Hans Tilkowski ensured England the title of World Champions. His second and third goals are among the most disputed and talked about in football: The 'over the line' crossbar shot when team mate Hunt turned to celebrate, convinced it was a goal, with referee and linesman confirming so. Hurst's hat-trick goal has entered football folklore with supporters running onto the pitch, prompting commentator Kenneth Wolstenholme to remark "They think it's all over... it is now!" as Geoff rocketed in his third and England's fourth to beat West Germany by 4-2 after extra-time.

More than anything, Geoff Hurst's goals had won the World Cup!

Two years later he scored England's second goal versus the Soviet Union (2-0) in Rome in the third-place play-off match as England finished in 3rd place in the 1968 European Championships. In Mexico 1970 he netted a World Cup winner versus Romania, before England were knocked out in the quarter-finals by old rivals West Germany.

Hurst's final and 49th cap was against familiar opponents in a 3-1 defeat to West Germany at Wembley in April 1972. He scored 24 international goals, including his first goal in his second cap versus Scotland at Hampden Park in a 4-3 victory. His 'other' England hat-trick was in a 5-0 friendly victory versus France at Wembley in March 1969.

If Geoff Hurst had never scored his famous hat-trick, he would still make our 50 Greatest Goalscorers. With 210 top-flight league goals he is among the 29 players who have over 200 in English football's top division and is 7th on the post-war list.

As a teenager as part of the Academy of Football at West Ham United he was initially played at centre-back and left back. He was given his First Division debut by Ted Fenton in February 1960 but was switched from midfield to centre-forward 'target man' by new manager Ron Greenwood. In season 1962/63 he scored a goal every other game.

In 1963/64 he scored seven goals in the FA Cup run, including the third goal versus Manchester United in the semi-final (3-1) and the crucial equaliser in the final 3-2 victory over Preston North End, with West Ham winning the cup for the first time in club history.

The following season, he scored in the shared Charity Shield draw with Liverpool at Anfield. In Europe, he helped West Ham win the European Cup Winners' Cup, beating German side 1860 Munich at Wembley.

In season 1965/66 Hurst scored a personal best of 40 goals. 23 in the league, including a hat-trick versus Newcastle United in a 4-3 victory at Upton Park. He scored 17 goals in cup competitions. 11 came in the League Cup, including in both semi-final legs versus Cardiff City. The Hammers lost over two legs in the final to West Brom Albion with Geoff and his team mates receiving a tankard!

A further 35 goals followed in season 1966/67. Even though West Ham had World Cup winners Hurst, Bobby Moore and Martin Peters, their highest league finish during this time was 8th in 1968/69. In October 1968, Hurst scored 6 league goals versus Sunderland in a club record 8-0 win, the double hat-trick equalling the club record from some 40 years earlier, set by Hammers leading goalscorer Vic Watson. Geoff still holds the record as the most recent scorer of a double hat-trick in the history of English top-flight football.

He was Voted Hammer of the Year three times. Geoff Hurst: 248 goals in 499 appearances for West Ham United, including 68 goals in cup competitions. He is the joint record scorer in League Cup history with Ian Rush on 49 goals.

In 1972 he moved to Stoke City, teaming up with fellow World Cup winner Gordon Banks. As always, Geoff had immaculate timing, scoring Stoke's first ever goal in Europe versus German opposition, Kaiserslautern FC. At the Victoria Ground he recorded 30 league goals in

108 appearances. There followed a final fling with WBA in the Second Division with 2 league goals in 10 appearances. He also enjoyed a time with Seattle Sounders, Stateside.

His managerial career took in Telford, Chelsea and Kuwait Sporting Club, before forging a new career in the world of business and insurance.

Hurst was knighted in 1998 and is forever a legend in West Ham claret and blue and England's three lions.

The day after his World Cup final hat-trick he was at home mowing the lawn. He recalled, "There are so many memories and that's the great thing about sport, that the memories last forever." With Geoff actively part of the Dementia in Football Campaign in 2021 as Ambassador for Alzheimer Society UK, he shall always be remembered as Geoff Hurst who give us one of the greatest of our memories.

Denis Law

The footballers' favourite footballer. Everyone looked to 'The Lawman', with razor sharp reflexes and the ability to hang in the air, his naturally charismatic playing style attracted attention and admiration among supporters, managers and fellow professionals.

"Denis was the best in the business, up there with the all-time greats. Electric. As a bloke and as a pal he's different class." – George Best.

"For my generation, Denis was every Scottish boy's hero." – Kenny Dalglish

"Without hesitation, I would name Denis Law as my favourite footballer of all time. In my eyes, Denis could do no wrong. He was magic." – Jimmy Greaves.

Born in Aberdeen, Law initially played at full back, before being moved to the forward line by his school teacher Mr Wright. He showed great promise and was selected for Scotland Schoolboys.

Spotted by fellow Scot and local man Archie Beattie, brother of Huddersfield Town manager Andy, he was invited for a trial and had an operation to correct a squint.

He was given his League debut by Beattie's replacement Bill Shankly on Christmas Eve 1956, aged sixteen, in a Second Division match versus Notts County. Two days later on Boxing Day, in the reverse league fixture versus County he scored his first football league goal in a 3-0 home victory.

Less than two years later, in October 1958 he was awarded his first international cap by Scotland and Manchester United manager Matt Busby, scoring on debut in a 3-0 win versus Wales at Ninian Park, Cardiff. In December 1959, Shanks was appointed manager of Liverpool and tried to sign the young Denis, but Liverpool did not have the sufficient funds.

The following spring in March 1960, a month after his 20th birthday, he signed for Manchester City for a British record fee of £55,000. On his City debut he scored in the 4-3 league defeat to Leeds at Elland Road and scored two vital goals in a 4-1 win versus Aston Villa to guarantee First Division football at Maine Road for the upcoming 1960/61 season.

During his time at Maine Road, he scored a record six goals in the FA Cup in January 1961, away to Luton Town, but the match was abandoned due to a water-logged pitch and all the goals were removed from the records. In the 3-1 replay defeat, he scored again.

After just a year with City, the adventure of a lucrative move to Italy proved too much to resist and he became the first six-figure British transfer – £125,000 to Torino in the summer of 1961.

Law took to the country of Italy, but the man-to-man marking was not to his liking. He stayed for a single season – 10 Serie A league goals in 27 appearances, though he did say he learned how to look after himself on the field of play after his experience. He was also involved in a car accident with team mate and English striker Joe Baker.

In the summer of 1962 for a third British record fee of £115,000 he was on his way to play in the red of Manchester United, signed by Matt Busby. Already an established international, you could say that, with the knowledge gained from his time abroad, both player and club were about to benefit in a big way, and it proved so. In his first season he scored on his league debut in August 1962 in a 2-2 draw with West Bromwich Albion at Old Trafford and he also hit four in a 5-3 away win at reigning champions Ipswich Town.

Over the next 11 seasons he was 'The King', with 237 goals, including 171 league goals in 309 league appearances and a club record 18 hat-tricks.

His first success was the 1963 FA Cup. He hit a hat-trick versus Huddersfield in a 5-0 win and scored the only goal of the game versus Southampton in the semi-final. At Wembley he found the net again in a 3-1 victory over Leicester City. Throughout his career he hit 41 FA Cup goals (third on the all-time list) from only 61 games.

In the 1962/63 season, cup winners United had just survived relegation, finishing 19th in the 22 club First Division. In May 1963, in the Manchester derby at Maine Road, Denis won a penalty (converted by Albert Quixall) to equalise and earn United a point and virtually send City down to the Second Division.

1963/64 was a personal triumph – 30 league goals with a club record 46 in total, including 15 goals in 11 games. In October 1963 (to celebrate the 100th anniversary of the Football Association) he was selected to represent the Rest of the World team versus England at Wembley, where he played alongside Di Stefano and Eusebio and scored his side's goal in a 2-1 defeat.

To top it all, he was named European Footballer of the Year. The King was now suitably crowned, though even halos slip. Throughout his career he was sent off three times (for feisty on-pitch behaviour) with bans – at the time that could mean a 28-day playing suspension without wages.

As Manchester United captain and top scorer his goals shot the club to league titles in 1964/65 (with 28 league goals, including four in a 7-0 victory over Aston Villa) and 1966/67, with 23 league goals including a double versus West Ham (6-1) at Upton Park in May 1967 to confirm the championship. All that remained now was to conquer Europe.

His goalscoring record in European competition was up there with the best on the continent, with 28 goals for United in Europe. Unfortunately, injury robbed him of playing in the 1968 European Cup Final, when United beat Benfica 4-1 at Wembley. The following season he did his utmost to retain the trophy as the season's leading scorer with nine in the European Cup but suffered defeat at the semi-final stage to eventual winners AC Milan.

At international level he was equally prolific. Over sixteen years he scored a joint record 30 international goals, including three hat-tricks for Scotland in 55 appearances. He scored the opening goal in the famous 3-2 victory over England (having been undefeated in 19 matches) at Wembley in April 1967, with Scotland now claiming to be the new 'unofficial' World Champions! The previous summer he had not watched the World Cup Final, preferring to play golf! His final cap was versus Zaire in Dortmund, West Germany at the World Cup Finals in 1974. Denis said of his international career: "Playing for Scotland is, without doubt, the greatest honour anybody could ever have bestowed on me."

At representative level, Law also played for the Football League versus the Italian League and for the Italian League versus the Football League.

With injuries restricting his game time with Manchester United and Matt Busby retired, he was given a free transfer, returning to Manchester City for the start of the 1973/74 season. One of the last hurrahs for United, with Best, Law and Charlton all playing together in red was in May 1971 with a 4-3 victory at Maine Road, when all three of 'the old boys' scored.

His 'final goal' in football was a back-heeled shot for City versus United at Old Trafford, with United already confirmed as relegated (City themselves finished only four points above the relegation zone). This time there would be no trademark arm in the air, hand clutching sleeve, finger point to the sky, he was a desolate figure as The King left his stage. In two spells with City, he scored 30 league goals in 68 appearances.

This was in fact not Law's 'final goal' in football or his final game. At the start of the 1974/75 season, he played for City in two Texaco Cup matches, scoring one goal. His 'final goal' was at Bramall Lane versus Sheffield United in a 4-2 defeat in August 1974, with his final game at Maine Road, four days later versus Oldham Athletic in a 2-1 victory.

English league record: 217 league goals in 458 league appearances, with 201 league goals in the top flight.

"No other player scored so many miracle goals as Denis Law." – Sir Matt Busby.

After his playing days for about a year he sold carpets, employed by a friend and Manchester United fan. Then, in 1975, he was offered work in the media and has been a popular pundit and presenter on both ITV and on BBC Radio and Television. Since 2010 he has been Patron of Football Aid.

In 2020, *The Lawman* documentary showcased his talents, reminding everyone why he is the one footballer with two statues at Old Trafford. One as part of the Holy Trinity (Best, Law, Charlton) and one at the Stretford End dedicated to The King, whom even fellow footballers look up to!

Nat Lofthouse

There's a wonderful photograph of Nat Lofthouse being carried shoulder high by his Bolton team mates holding the FA Cup above his head, almost as if in the picture, Nat is touching the sky with the gleaming old trophy.

The year is 1958, a moment in time capturing a Wembley scene of happiness and jubilation. Captain Lofthouse has just scored both goals for his hometown club to defeat Manchester United 2-0 to record Bolton Wanderers' fourth and to date most recent Cup Final triumph.

Just seven weeks earlier he had dislocated his collarbone and bet his manager Bill Ridding £1 he could still make Wembley for the Cup Final.

After the match, Nat said, "My collarbone felt champion – never a twinge." During the match, Nat shot Bolton into the lead after two minutes and, before the hour mark, he shoulder charged United keeper Harry Gregg into the net to make it two nil. Controversy surrounded the incident but the goal stood and Bolton and Nat had won the cup.

It had been tough for Bolton, with all the nation behind Manchester United following the Munich Air Disaster three months earlier, but United manager Matt Busby graciously said, "The better team won, there's no doubt about that."

For Lofthouse and Bolton Wanderers FC it was the greatest day of their footballing lives, which made up for the disappointment of their Wembley appearance five years earlier.

In the 1953 cup run, Nat scored in every round. In the semi-final at Maine Road his two goals in a 4-3 victory over Everton sent Bolton to the final. In the decider versus Blackpool, he found the net again as the Trotters led 3-1, but the two Stanleys, Matthews and Mortensen, turned the game upside down and the Seasiders won 4-3 in the highest scoring 20th century Cup Final.

The joy of his two goals in the 1958 Cup Final win had made up for all the heartache and was reward for a lifetime of service and loyalty.

Nathaniel Lofthouse was Bolton born and bred, scoring goals for the same Castle Hill school team as another Bolton born goalscoring legend, Tommy Lawton.

He was signed as a 14-year-old apprentice in 1939. He made his debut in wartime football and was a Bevin Boy, working down the coal mines. "The job proved to be the best I could possibly have had, it made me fitter... I learnt to take hard knocks without feeling them, my legs became stronger and when I played football I felt I was shooting with greater power." Having been underground, Lofthouse was offered professional terms with Bolton in 1946, the same year that 33 fans lost their lives in the Burnden Park tragedy.

A one club man, happy to be a 'Wanderer', with 503 appearances, 285 goals in all competitions. 452 league appearances with 255 league goals, all in the First Division, places Lofthouse 8th on the all-time list of top-flight goalscorers in English football history. In post-war football, his 255 league goals constitutes a record tally for a single club at the highest level. Devoted to Bolton Wanderers FC, in December 1947 he combined the two great loves of his life, marrying his sweetheart Alma in the morning and at Burnden Park in the afternoon he scored twice in a Bolton 3-2 win over Wolves!

For England he earned 33 international caps, scoring 30 goals, including twice on debut in November 1950 versus Yugoslavia. At the 1954 World Cup in Switzerland he scored three times – twice versus Belgium (4-4) and once in the quarter-final defeat to Uruguay (4-2) at the St. Jakob Stadium, Basel. His most famous goals for his country were in the match billed as the game to crown the 'unofficial European Champions' versus Austria in May 1952. Displaying characteristic bravery, he scored twice in a 3-2 victory and was dubbed the 'Lion of Vienna'. Three days later he scored another double versus Switzerland, winning 3-0 in Zurich. He also scored twice versus Scotland in April 1955, as England beat the auld enemy at Wembley for the first time since 1934, with a resounding 7-2 victory.

Lofthouse was awarded Footballer of the Year in 1953 and was the First Division top scorer for the 1955/56 season with 33 league goals, including seven goals in one week in December 1955: four goals versus Birmingham City (6-0) and a hat-trick versus Chelsea (4-0).

In the 1958/59 season, he scored 35 goals as Bolton finished 4th, their highest league position since 1926/27. In October 1958, in the Charity Shield, he played in goal for ten minutes, covering for an injured goalkeeper and he still had time to score twice in the 4-1 victory at Burnden Park over League Champions Wolves. Nat was revered!

Bobby Charlton said, "The first time I saw a professional game was at Newcastle and Nat Lofthouse was playing. He was a leader, he had fantastic ability in the air, and he was strong, he was a talisman."

When Bolton moved from their Burnden Park ground to the new Reebok Stadium in 1997, a stand was renamed the Nat Lofthouse Stand in his honour. In 2013 a statue was unveiled to commemorate Nat's devotion as a player, scout, coach, manager, club president and, above all, supporter. Nat represented the very best of the people of Bolton and Bolton Wanderers Football Club.

A lion-hearted man who welcomed you with the friendly greeting, "Just call me Lofty."

Jackie Milburn

In the black and white stripes of Newcastle United, Jackie Milburn was the club's record goalscorer until Alan Shearer scored his 201st goal for the Magpies in February 2006. Jackie's son Jack, who had written *Jackie Milburn: A Man of Two Halves*, said; "They would have complemented each other well... they would have made a great fantasy football partnership. Dad wasn't as physical as Alan, but he was catch-me-if-you-can quick and scored most of his goals from 20 or 30 yards."

Wor Jackie, whose initials JET (John Edward Thompson) truly reflected his blistering turn of pace. It is documented that Milburn has 200 goals in 397 appearances for Newcastle but, taking into account his record in the Charity Shield (a fixture often overlooked among goalscoring records), he actually scored 201 goals. In the annual curtain raiser, he found the net in September 1951 versus Spurs at White Hart Lane.

Milburn's full record for Newcastle reads: League appearances 353, league goals 177; FA Cup 44 games, 23 goals; and Charity Shield 2 games 1 goal. (He also scored another 38 goals in wartime matches.)

It all started for the young Milburn when he replied to an advertisement in a local paper. Newcastle had invited players for a trial at St. James Park. Jackie took up the story: "The Toon give me a game in midweek when I was lucky enough to score two goals." For the second trial: "Long before the 2pm kick-off I arrived at the ground with my boots in a brown paper parcel and sat outside eating a couple of pies for my dinner." Milburn scored six goals and was signed up to play in wartime matches while continuing his job as a fitter in a colliery.

As a youngster he was a talented athlete, especially the sprints and was played on the left wing. In his professional debut for the Geordies in January 1946 he scored twice versus Barnsley in the FA Cup.

As league fixtures resumed in 1946/47, Milburn was switched to centre-forward as Newcastle ran up a club record and still the biggest margin of victory in a match in England's top two divisions – 13-0 versus Newport County in October 1946 in the Second Division, with Jackie scoring twice. In season 1947/48 Newcastle won promotion back to the First Division.

In October 1948 he scored on his England debut versus Northern Ireland in a 6-2 win at Windsor Park in Belfast. In total he won 13 international caps scoring 10 goals, including a hat-trick versus Wales in October 1949 in a 4-1 victory at Ninian Park, Cardiff. He also scored in friendly internationals versus Argentina and Portugal and in 1950 he played in his country's first World Cup, making an appearance in the group stage versus Spain.

Although his goalscoring contemporaries Nat Lofthouse and Stan Mortensen won more international caps, in season 1950/51 Milburn achieved something neither Morty nor Lofty or countless other goalscorers have. He won the FA Cup with Newcastle, scoring in every round including the final, a feat only accomplished by a handful of players in the history of the competition. In the semi-final, after a goal-less first match, he scored in the replay versus Wolves. In the Cup Final, Jackie scored both goals in a 2-0 victory over Blackpool. The second a long-range shot described by Stanley Matthews as "the greatest goal I have ever seen".

The following season, Newcastle became the first club in the 20th century to retain the cup, beating Arsenal one nil. The same 1951/52 season saw Milburn score 25 league goals including in both Tyne Wear derbies versus Sunderland as part of a club record 98 goals in the league.

In 1955, the cup was won for the third time in five seasons with Milburn scoring at the time the quickest cup final goal in a record 45 seconds, heading past Manchester City keeper Bert Trautman in a 3-1 win over City.

Injuries started to limit his appearances for Newcastle and in June 1957, a month after his 33rd birthday, he accepted an offer to become player/manager of Linfield Football Club in the Irish League. In just over three seasons in Northern Ireland he won nine trophies including the 1960 Irish Cup, scoring twice in a 5-1 win versus Ards at the Oval. Jackie also scored Linfield's first goal in Europe, netting both in a famous 2-1 win over Gothenburg at Windsor Park in September 1959.

There followed a spell as manager of Ipswich Town, where the pressures of work led Milburn to a battle with the bottle and post football he worked in a scrapyard before a new career in sports journalism.

A humble, modest, genuine sportsman, from a footballing family (Charlton brothers, Jack and Bobby were cousins) Milburn was plagued by a lack of self-belief, for all the adulation during his playing days. Ultimately, he knew how much he meant to supporters, especially those in his native North East when a bumper crowd turned out for his testimonial match in 1967. Now in the 21st century Milburn is forever remembered with the Milburn Stand and Wor Jackie statue at St. James Park.

In the words of Alan Shearer, "When I was growing up everybody talked about Jackie Milburn. To see my name alongside the great Jackie Milburn is a great honour for me."

Stan Mortensen

In 140 FA Cup Finals over 150 years, three footballers have scored a hat-trick in the cup final. Billy Townley for Blackburn Rovers in 1890, Jimmy Logan for Notts County in 1894 and Stanley Harding Mortensen for Blackpool versus Bolton Wanderers on Saturday 2nd May 1953.

For eternity Morty shall be the one to have done so in the 20th century and to date he remains the one to have achieved the feat at Wembley Stadium. In itself, it is remarkable and when you consider the names on the list who have scored twice on the showpiece occasion it is elevated further among the game's greatest achievements. Lofthouse, Milburn, Rush and Wright are among those with two, but in the record books, the one and only Mortensen has three beside his name, with many of the game's greatest goalscorers having never scored twice, or once, never mind three times!

Born on Tyneside, as a teenager he was signed by Blackpool as an apprentice in 1938. With the outbreak of World War Two he was stationed at RAF Lossiemouth in North-east Scotland as a wireless operator and gunner on bombing missions with the Royal Air Force.

On one occasion he was very lucky to escape with his life after the Wellington Bomber he was in crashed and killed two crew members. Once recovered he represented Aberdeen in war-time fixtures. Popular at Pittodrie, he scored on debut and was heralded as a 'flier' for his speed off the mark. When posted back to England he also guested for Arsenal, before returning to Blackpool as football restarted after the war.

The FA Cup resumed in 1946 and, now aged 25, Morty began his football league career with the resumption of league football for the 1946/47 season. Over ten seasons his goalscoring saw the Tangerines enjoy the most successful time in the club's history, winning silverware and challenging for the league.

In 1948 he scored in every round of the FA Cup including the final (one of only twelve players to have done so). In the semi-final versus Spurs (3-1) he scored a hat-trick, as the Seasiders reached their first cup final and in the defeat in the final, 4-2 by Manchester United, he scored Blackpool's second goal.

In season 1950/51 Morty's goals saw Blackpool going for the 'double' but they suffered further cup final heartache, losing to Newcastle United and finishing third in the league, at the time their highest ever league placing. Mortensen was the First Division top scorer with 30 league goals, during which time he had a post-war record run of scoring in 11 consecutive top-flight matches – only equalled in 2015/16 by Jamie Vardy of Leicester City. Stan actually scored in 15 consecutive league games in which he played (he missed matches in the run due to injury). He also has just as impressive streak in the FA Cup, scoring in 12 consecutive rounds, including the 1948 final.

By now he was an established international, having represented his country in war-time games. For England he scored 23 goals in 25 matches and was involved in some of the most famous games of all time. In spectacular fashion on debut, he hit a record four goals in a 10-0 away win versus Portugal in Lisbon in May 1947. He also scored hat-tricks versus Sweden at Highbury (4-2) and in Belfast versus Northern Ireland (6-2). In a 4-0 win in Turin the following year versus Italy he scored as part of arguably the greatest forward line in history: Mortensen, Matthews, Lawton, Finney and Mannion.

At England's first World Cup in Brazil in 1950, Morty scored his nation's first goal in a World Cup Finals in a 2-0 victory versus Chile at the Maracana Stadium in Rio. He also played in the shock one-nil defeat to the USA.

In his last year as an international he scored in the 4-4 game for England versus a Rest of Europe side in the FA's 90th anniversary match in October 1953. A month later he found the net again in the 3-6 home defeat to Hungary, as Ferenc Puskas' Magical Magyars became the first foreign side to win at Wembley.

1953 was indeed a historic year. Tenzing and Hillary reached the top of Everest and Morty scaled the heights at Wembley with his memorable hat-trick. Along with Stanley Matthews' wing wizardry he had turned the cup final around, winning 4-3 after Bolton had led 3-1. Dubbed 'The Matthews Final', the man himself said 'a Stanley Final', "Stan Mortensen got a hat-trick," as Blackpool Football Club won the cup for the first and to date one time in their history in one of the most exciting finals Wembley has witnessed.

Player and club had reached their pinnacle. Two years later, as knee injuries took their toll on his playing time, Morty departed. For Blackpool he scored 197 league goals, all in the top flight, in 317 league appearances. He finished his league career in the lower divisions with Hull City (18 league goals in 42 appearances) and with Southport (10 league goals in 36 appearances). A career total of 225 league goals.

He was Blackpool manager for two years from 1967 and also ran a sports shop in the town. In 2005, Blackpool FC unveiled a statue of Morty at their Bloomfield Road Stadium; a deserving tribute to a Wembley hat-trick war hero.

Arthur Rowley

In the history of British football, George Arthur Rowley has scored more league goals than anyone.

In his goalscoring lifetime he surpassed the English records of Steve Bloomer and Dixie Dean, Anglo/Scottish of Hughie Gallacher and Scottish of Jimmy McGrory.

When he retired in 1965, he had 434 league goals from 619 appearances. To put that into some kind of perspective, in the years since only two players, Jimmy Greaves and John Aldridge, have come within 100 goals of Arthur Rowley's total.

It is a factual observation that all of Greavsie's 357 league goals came in the top flight of English football while Rowley's 434 were spread across the four divisions of the Football League, with 51 of his league goals scored over three seasons in the top flight. This should not detract from the significance of one of the most enduring goalscoring records in European club football.

He remains the one player in over 130 years of English league football to have over 400 league goals and as the Football League website states: "Arthur Rowley stands head and shoulders above anybody in league history for goalscoring."

From a footballing family, his father was a goalkeeper for Walsall. In 1941, young Arthur, just turned 15, played alongside his older brother Jack in a war-time fixture for Manchester United.

A year later he signed amateur forms with his hometown club Wolverhampton Wanderers. After his military service he joined rivals West Brom Albion. In 24 league appearances at The Hawthorns, he scored four goals and was then transferred to Fulham in December 1948.

He began to blossom and his 19 goals earned promotion to the top flight for the first time in Fulham's history as Second Division champions in 1948/49. After one season with Fulham in the First Division and 27 league goals in 56 appearances, Leicester City paid a club record fee of £14,000 to take Rowley to Filbert Street.

The 'Gunner' started with a goal on debut. In eight seasons from 1950/51 to 1957/58 inclusive he notched up 251 league goals from 303 appearances, a strike rate of 2½ goals every 3 games.

A reliable penalty taker, he averaged over 30 league goals a season. In season 1952/53 he was the league top scorer with 39 league goals. The following campaign he scored 30 league goals as the Foxes won the Second Division Championship with every goal counting, as Leicester won the division on goal average.

Despite Rowley's 23 First Division goals, Leicester were relegated, but were Second Division Champs again in 1956/57 under the management of David Halliday with Arthur excelling as overall leading league scorer again with a club record 44 league goals.

Staying loyal to Leicester he resisted approaches from the big clubs of the day. Although he was never capped at the highest level by his country, he did make one appearance for England 'B' in 1956, scoring in a 4-1 victory versus Switzerland. He also represented the Football League versus the Irish League.

In his final season with Leicester in 1957/58, his 20 league goals in

25 games kept City in the First Division.

Aged 32, in the summer of 1958 he was appointed the player/manager of Fourth Division Shrewsbury Town. On arrival, he said he "would rather win 5-4 than 1-0".

True to his word, in his first season (1958/59) he would lead a goalscoring revolution, a club record of 101 league goals with Rowley scoring a club record 38 league goals as the division's top scorer, culminating with the Shrews winning promotion for the first time in club history.

He was now arguably Shropshire's most renowned resident since Charles Darwin, who exactly 100 years earlier in 1859 had started his own revolutionary evolution. Under Rowley's stewardship Shrewsbury held their own in the Third Division and in 1960/61 reached the semi-finals of a cup competition for the first time in their history. After a famous victory over Everton in the quarter-finals they were defeated over two legs by Rotherham United in the last four of the inaugural League Cup.

Rowley played on before retiring at the end of the 1964/65 season. His figures at Gay Meadow: a club record 152 league goals in 236 league appearances.

He continued as manager for three more seasons with Shrewsbury, before leading Southend United to their first ever promotion in 1971/72.

He is the one player to hold the single season league scoring record for two separate English league clubs – Leicester City and Shrewsbury Town.

Rowley was a quiet, humble man and perhaps among all his goalscoring records the most endearing is from 22nd October 1955 when Arthur and his brother Jack both scored their 200th league goal, Arthur for Leicester City and Jack for Plymouth Argyle. A memorable milestone where the stars aligned perfectly for footballing brotherly love.

Bobby Smith

In season 1960/61 Bobby Smith's goals won Tottenham Hotspur the League Championship and FA Cup – 'the glorious double'. The thunderbolt frontman struck 33 goals, 28 in the league and 5 in the cup, with Spurs becoming the first club side to win the double in the 20th century and only the third in English Football history after Preston North End and Aston Villa. With 208 goals from 317 matches, Smith spearheaded Spurs 'Glory Glory years' at home and in Europe.

Robert Alfred Smith was from Lingdale, North Yorkshire. After leaving school he joined his father working at the local ironstone mine as an apprentice blacksmith. For recreation he played football for Redcar Albion and Redcar Boys Club, initially as a full-back before covering in at centre-forward. Making an immediate impact up front, he was signed by Chelsea as an amateur and was placed with one of their junior sides, Tudor Rose.

In the 1950 London FA Youth Cup Final, Smith scored a hat-trick for Chelsea v Spurs at Stamford Bridge. He made his league debut aged 17, scoring 7 goals in 16 league appearances in the 1950/51 season to help Chelsea avoid relegation on goal average. In 1952 he hit another cup treble, this time versus Leeds United and John Charles in a FA Cup replay. With Smith balancing football and National Service with the Medical Corps he found it difficult to establish himself in the first team and did not play enough games to earn a championship medal in 1954/55.

Looking for a fresh start he left Chelsea after 23 league goals in 74 games, signing for Spurs for a bargain £16,000 in December 1955. Now playing regularly under manager Jimmy Anderson, he scored twice on Christmas Day 1956 in a 6-0 victory over Everton as Spurs finished the season as runners-up to Manchester United.

In season 1957/58 he was the First Division top scorer with 36 league goals, including five goals versus Aston Villa in March 1958. In October 1958 he hit four in a 10-4 victory over Everton in Bill Nicholson's first match in charge. The following season, Bobby scored four again in a club record 13-2 win in a FA cup replay versus Crewe Alexander in February 1960.

The glorious double season began with Smith scoring 13 league goals as Spurs won a record 11 consecutive First Division matches, finishing on 66 points (two points for win), equalling the Arsenal league points record from 1930/31.

As top scorer with 28 league goals, he contributed to a record 115 top-flight league goals, most memorably scoring twice in the 4-2 victory over Arsenal in the North London derby and also in the game that clinched the league title in April with a 2-1 win over nearest challengers Sheffield Wednesday. In the cup, Smith scored twice in the 3-0 semi-final win over reigning champions Burnley at Villa Park. In Tottenham's first Wembley final he opened the scoring in a 2-0 triumph over Leicester City.

A year later, he was back at Wembley, once again finding the net as Spurs retained the FA Cup, beating Burnley 3-1. Smith is the only player to score in consecutive FA Cup Finals in the 20th century for a winning side. The same 1961/62 season, he scored in both semi-final legs versus Benfica in Spurs' first European campaign, and also had a crucial goal dubiously ruled out for offside, costing a place in the European Cup Final.

The next season, 1962/63 in Europe, he scored in the Battle of Britain tie with Rangers and again in a European semi-final versus OFK Belgrade, Spurs going onto lift the European Cup Winners' Cup to become the first British club side to win a European trophy, beating Athletic Madrid 5-1. Once again, Bobby Smith, manager Bill Nicholson, captain Danny Blanchflower et al had made history.

1963/64 would be Smith's final season at White Hart Lane. He departed as the club's all-time record goalscorer (until overtaken by team mate Jimmy Greaves) with 176 league goals from 271 league appearances.

During his Spurs career he was capped 15 times by England, scoring 13 goals, including 8 in his first 5 internationals. He scored on his debut in October 1960 versus Northern Ireland (5-2) and in the same month hit two doubles versus Luxembourg (9-0) and Spain (4-2). The highlight was a famous 9-3 Wembley win versus Scotland in April 1961 when Bobby scored twice.

With new club Brighton his 19 league goals in 31 appearances helped the Seagulls win the Fourth Division Championship in 1964/65. With Smith having issues with his weight and fitness he departed Brighton and went into non-league football with Hastings United and Banbury United.

His football league record reads: Goals 218, games 376, including 199 league goals in the top flight, just one shy of the 200 club.

In the 1970s he featured in charity matches and guested in testimonials and had driving jobs and was a painter and decorator. Living nearby, Bobby was a welcome and regular visitor to White Hart Lane, all generations of Tottenham fans knowing those 'Glory Glory years' would not have been possible without the bravery and commitment of their swashbuckling centre-forward.

In 2002, *My Memories of Spurs* was published, the recollections of a goalscoring Number 9.

1970s & 1980s

The 1976/77 season saw the Football League follow Scotland (who by this time had established a new Scottish Premier League in 1975/76) by replacing goal average with goal difference.

Back in the 1970s goalscoring was not exactly going out of fashion, but there was certainly a lack of goals per game compared to the previous decades. There was no shortage though of stylish strikers to entertain. As well as your fans' favourites, poachers now had club sponsorship on shirts, pioneered by Coventry City and Derby County as the 1970s began new trends. With television technology supporters could now see their goals in colour on *Match of the Day* on a Saturday night and *The Big Match* on a Sunday afternoon.

Into the 1980s, match day attendances reached their lowest levels since the end of World War Two due to a combination of the economy and hooliganism. Perhaps with this in mind, to generate interest, the Football League introduced 3 points for a win for the start of the 1981/82 season. The importance of winning football matches was now more significant than ever.

Goalscorers of the time included:

Charlie George, whose FA Cup Final scorcher helped Arsenal win the double in 1971.

Mick Channon and his trademark windmill arm goal celebration, with 300 plus career goals, including 228 for Southampton and 21 for England.

Peter Osgood, the King of Stamford Bridge who scored goals for Chelsea in the finals of the League Cup, FA Cup and European Cup Winners' Cup.

Elvis Presley fan, Frank Worthington, with over 250 club goals including for Bolton Wanderers versus Ipswich Town during the 1978/79 season, when *The Big Match* cameras captured his memorable goal – playing keepy uppy then flicking the ball over the onrushing defence and volleying home.

The telepathic Anfield partnership between John Toshack and Kevin Keegan. Toshack, Keegan, one nil! Mighty Mouse scored over 250 club goals for Scunthorpe United, Liverpool, Hamburg SV, Southampton and Newcastle, with a further 21 for England who he also managed. Tosh – over 200 club goals for Cardiff City, Liverpool and Swansea City, with a further 13 for Wales who he also managed.

Tony 'Bomber' Brown, a wing half and inside forward with over 200 league goals for WBA who, like a number of players at this time, experienced playing in the United States.

Tony Kellow, Exeter City record scorer with 150 goals in three spells with The Grecians.

Keith Edwards and Tommy Tynan whose careers ran parallel from the mid-1970s through to the early 1990s, each with over 250 League goals.

Moustached Bob Hatton with over 200 goals at nine clubs through the leagues. Another nine-club man was Ernie Moss, Chesterfield's record league scorer with 161 goals across three spells.

Dixie McNeill at Hereford United, the Football League's leading scorer for two consecutive seasons 1974/75 and 1975/76.

Derek Hales with over 150 goals for Charlton (many in partnership with Mike Flanagan).

Trevor Francis, the first 1 million-pound footballer when transferred from Birmingham City to Nottingham Forest in February 1979 and three months later scored the only goal of the game to win the European Cup.

Tony Adcock, 200 plus league goals, over half for Colchester United.

Luther Blissett with over 150 League goals for Watford, including as First Division top scorer in 1982/83 and a hat-trick on his full England debut.

Alan Buckley who was prolific for Walsall in the 1970s, later managing the club and also Grimsby Town.

Welsh International, Gordon 'Ivor' Davies, Fulham's record scorer with 178 goals.

Goalscoring winger David Moss, with over 150 goals for the Towns – Swindon and Luton.

Micky Quinn – over 200 league goals across the Football league.

Simon Garner – 194 goals as Blackburn Rovers record scorer.

Trevor Senior, Reading FC record scorer with 191 league and cup goals.

Brian McClair, who scored over 100 goals in Scotland and England for Celtic and Manchester United respectively.

Mo Johnston – over 200 career goals, including for both Celtic and Rangers.

Alan Smith twice topped the scoring charts in England with Arsenal and also scored in the famous Brian Moore commentary "It's up for grabs now" match at Anfield in May 1989.

Frankie Bunn holds the record for most goals scored in a League Cup match with six for Oldham Athletic versus Scarborough in October 1989. Frankie's team mate, attacking midfielder/striker, Roger Palmer is the club's top scorer with 157 goals.

Steve 'Chalkie' White. Throughout the 1980s and into the '90s over 200 league goals including for Bristol Rovers, Swindon Town and Hereford United.

Joe Harper, Aberdeen record scorer with 205 goals.

Derek Johnstone for Glasgow Rangers, 210 goals.

Charlie Nicholas for rivals Celtic, over 200 career goals, more than 100 for Celtic and scored both goals for Arsenal to win the 1987 League Cup final.

John Robertson of Hearts, a record scorer with 310 goals, also managed the club.

Willie Pettigrew had five clubs, with over 100 goals for Motherwell FC.

Paul Sturrock, in a one-club playing career, scored 171 goals for Dundee United and also managed the club.

John Aldridge

476 goals! John Aldridge is British football's record post-war goalscorer. 457 club goals and 19 international goals. With 329 league goals he is 6th on the all-time list in English league football. Taking into account his La Liga goals, his grand league total is 362.

He is one of only eleven players to have scored 300 or more league goals in the history of English football and the only one to have done so in the past half century.

A born and bred Scouser and lifelong supporter of Liverpool Football Club, as a schoolboy he was rejected by the Reds and began his goalscoring odyssey with local side South Liverpool whilst continuing to work as a toolmaker.

While impressing in non-league football he was signed for £3,500 by Newport County and was on his way to South Wales when he said, "Newport gave me my start in the game, the opportunity to do what I had always wanted to do, which was to play professional football."

In his debut season, 1979/80, under manager Len Ashurst, Newport won the Welsh Cup and were promoted from the Fourth Division, returning to the third tier of English football for the first time since 1962. The following season, in partnership with Tommy Tynan, Aldridge and Newport reached the quarter-finals of the European Cup Winners' Cup, losing out to eventual finalist Carl Zeiss Jena. In March 1984, Newport accepted an offer of £78,000 from Oxford United and after five years at Somerton Park with a scoring record of 69 league goals from 170 league appearances, Aldo was on his way to the Manor Ground.

In his time with the U's under the management of Jim Smith and latterly Maurice Evans and in strike partnership with Billy Hamilton, Aldo was a goalscoring sensation: 72 league goals in 114 appearances, with 90 goals in 141 games in total. The Third Division Championship was won at the end of his first two months at the club. In the 1984/85 season he was the Second Division top scorer with a club record 30 league goals as another title was secured.

In 1985/86, his first season in the top flight, he scored 23 league goals, leaving Oxford one point above the relegation zone and he also bagged another five goals en route to a first Wembley cup final. Under new manager Evans, Oxford beat previous boss Smith's Queen's Park Rangers 3-0 to win the League Cup, their first major trophy in club history. As Aldridge continued to score in the First Division, 15 league goals in 25 appearances by the New Year, his dream move happened in

January 1987 when Liverpool offered Oxford a club record fee of £750,000 as a replacement for the soon to be departing Ian Rush.

On his full debut he scored the only goal of the game versus Southampton at Anfield in February 1987. With new signings John Barnes and Peter Beardsley, Aldridge started 1987/88 in blistering form, scoring in each of the first nine league games of the season (which amounted to scoring in ten consecutive league games, a club record, as he had found the net in the final league game of the previous season), as Kenny Dalglish's side swept all before them. Rush was never in doubt, saying, "I always felt that John was the main man to take over from me."

The Reds went on a record equalling run, matching Leeds United's 29 league games undefeated from the start of a season in 1973/74. When Liverpool did lose, in their 30th league match of the season against Everton at Goodison Park in March 1988, Aldridge was missing through injury. The only goal of the game was scored by Wayne Clarke, younger brother of Leeds' Allan.

He topped the First Division goalscoring charts with 26 league goals as the Reds lifted the league title. Going for the double, in the FA Cup semi-final he scored both goals in a 2-1 victory over Nottingham Forest at Hillsborough. In the final, normally so deadly from 12 yards, Aldo became the first player to have a penalty saved in a FA Cup Final at Wembley, when Dave Beasant denied him and Wimbledon won the cup. Three months later, in the Charity Shield, he scored twice in a 2-1 victory over the Dons, exacting, some sort of redemption.

In season 1988/89 he added 31 goals in league and cup, as again Liverpool chased the double. Returning to Hillsborough for another FA Cup semi-final, again versus Forest, at 3.06pm on Saturday 15th April 1989, the game was halted as tragedy unfolded on the Leppings Lane terrace.

In the re-arranged match at Old Trafford, the Reds' Number 8 scored twice in a 3-1 win and in the all Merseyside final, after only four minutes he fastened onto a Steve McMahon through ball to shoot beyond Neville Southall with the Reds winning 3-2 after extra time. The following Friday, all Liverpool followers were left shell-shocked as Michael Thomas' last minute goal for Arsenal denied the club the double.

With the re-signed Rush now preferred up front, Aldo moved onto Real Sociedad in September 1989. His final act as a Liverpool player was to score from the penalty spot in a 9-0 win versus Crystal Palace after which he said, "To get the chance to score at the Kop End in my last game was special, it was a very poignant moment for me." At the end of the match, he threw his shirt and boots into the Kop. John Aldridge, Liverpool FC, 50 league goals in 83 appearances.

Aldridge was a record signing for the Spanish club £1.1m – 210 million pesetas. After initial scepticism, he was the first non-Basque player of the modern era, he was a runaway success at San Sebastian, helping achieve European qualification through the league. 'El Zorro' scored 33 La Liga goals in 63 appearances including at both the Bernabéu and the Nou Camp versus Real Madrid and Barcelona.

After two seasons Aldo returned home to Friday night football at Prenton Park, scoring twice on his league debut versus Brighton for Tranmere Rovers in August 1991, a month short of his 33rd birthday. Two months later he hit a hat-trick versus Newcastle United in the Zenith Data Systems Cup, Tranmere winning on penalties after the match finished 6-6 AET (Micky Quinn also scored a hat-trick for the visitors). Under manager Johnny King, Rovers reached the play-offs three times, just missing out on promotion to the Premier League. In 1993/94 Aldo scored in both legs of the League Cup semi-final, pushing Aston Villa all the way.

He was the second tier top scorer in seasons 1994/95 and 1995/96. Signing off in typical fashion in his final game for Tranmere, aged 39 years 228 days, he scored both goals in a 2-1 home win versus Wolves at the end of the 1997/98 season. By this stage he was player/manager and then manager until 2001, the highlight leading Tranmere to their first major final versus Leicester City in the 2000 League Cup. For the Super White Army he scored 138 league goals in 243 appearances, 174 goals in total.

As an adopted Irishman, he played international football for the Republic of Ireland, amassing 19 goals in 69 games (30 as a Tranmere player) under Jack Charlton, playing at Euro '88, World Cup '90 and scoring versus Mexico in the World Cup finals in USA '94.

Aldo did more than alright and is certainly as sound as a pound and is now as popular as ever in media, radio, television, and as a columnist. A Kopite and Kop Idol, the Scouser was a favourite of the fans wherever he played.

Clive Allen

'He only scores goals' was going to be the title of Clive Allen's autobiography. When released in 2019, the book was called *Up Front* with the original thought now Chapter Eight.

A skilful ball playing forward, he illustrated this perfectly for Tottenham Hotspur in the 1986/87 season, scoring a post-war top flight record of 49 league and cup goals, surpassing the personal bests of Jimmy Greaves, Denis Law and Ian Rush.

A natural born goalscorer, aged six he was playing for the under tens. His Dad Les was part of Spurs' double winning side and his younger brother Bradley and cousins Paul and Martin were all professionals. Aged 13, playing for Havering District, he was spotted by QPR scout Ron Howard. After leaving school he took up an apprenticeship with Rangers, serving his time with the youth team and reserves.

Given his full debut by Steve Burtenshaw in April 1979, he scored a hat-trick versus Coventry City a month short of his eighteenth birthday. In 1979/80, under Tommy Docherty, he hit 30 goals, 28 in the league, to be the Second Division top scorer and leading goalscorer for the season in the Football League.

Now the hottest young goalscorer around with 32 league goals in 49 appearances, he was the subject in the summer of 1980 of one of the most bizarre transfers of all time. In June he became the first £1million teenager, moving from QPR to Arsenal. Sixty-two days later and after playing three pre-season friendlies he was released by Arsenal manager Terry Neill and was on his way to Crystal Palace, managed by Terry Venables, for another seven figure fee as part of a swap deal involving Palace left back Kenny Sansom and keeper Paul Barron.

Joining the newly-promoted Eagles, hyped as the 'Team of the Eighties', during the 1980/81 season Clive would play for four different managers, including Venners and Malcolm Allison. Palace finished bottom of the First Division, 16 points adrift with only six wins all season from 42 league games. Allen continued to score with 9 league goals in 25 appearances.

By the start of the new season, he had left South London for up West, returning to Loftus Road, linking up again with Venables and playing on the Rs' artificial 'plastic pitch'. Clive scored seven goals in the Hoops' FA Cup run all the way to Wembley. He hit four in a replay versus Blackpool, scored the only goal of the game in the quarter-final versus old club Palace and did the same versus WBA, as fate would have it, in the semi-final at Highbury.

In the final, football fate would again play its part with the final versus Spurs. Allen had to withdraw into the second half after sustaining an injury in the first half. Having celebrated his 21st birthday on the Thursday before the final, it was a cruel blow and he also missed the replay as Spurs won the cup.

In 1982/83 he won promotion with QPR, as Second Division Champions, Allen grabbing a hat-trick on the magic carpet in a 6-1 win over Middlesborough. In March 1984 he scored one of the most memorable goals of the decade. On a muddy pitch versus West Ham United at Upton Park his famous drag-backs goal, fortunately captured by the TV cameras, has featured on many a greatest goals compilation.

In June he made his England debut on the Tour of South America versus Brazil in the Maracana in Rio, the 'John Barnes goal' game, and visited the Christ the Redeemer statue. In all he won five caps without scoring, his final appearance in February 1988 against Israel in Tel Aviv.

In that summer of '84 he also made the move of his career. After 40 league goals in 87 appearances in his second spell with QPR, Allen was on his way to Spurs for £700,000. He scored twice on his league debut in a 4-1 win over Everton at Goodison Park as Spurs finished the 1984/85 season in third place, their highest league position since the Martin Chivers side in 1970/71.

Very often playing as a lone striker in the 1986/87 season, he twice scored league hat-tricks, both 3-0 wins, away to Aston Villa on the opening day in August and at home to Norwich City in April. In David Pleat's all-star team alongside Mabbutt, Ardiles, Hoddle and Waddle, Spurs challenged on all fronts.

In the league, Allen scored 33 league goals, the highest in the top flight since Francis Lee for Manchester City in 1971/72 as Spurs again finished third. In the League Cup, he set a new competition record of 12 goals, including in both semi-final legs and replay defeat versus Arsenal. In the FA Cup he hit four, including in the semi-final versus Watford and the opening goal in the final, as Spurs lost 3-2 to Coventry City.

Silverware eluded Allen, but he received personal recognition – voted Footballer of the Year and PFA Player of the Year for the 1986/87 season as well as winning the Golden Boot as First Division top scorer. He was also the leading league goalscorer, the first player since Tommy Briggs in the 1950s (Grimsby Town and Blackburn Rovers), to have topped the league scoring charts with two separate clubs.

In August 1987 he represented the Football League versus the Rest of the World in the Centenary Match at Wembley. For Spurs he scored 60 league goals in 105 league games.

Allen's next challenge was swapping North London for the South of France in a £1million move to Bordeaux in Ligue 1, top scoring with 13 goals in 19 games, playing alongside Eric Cantona.

He then was involved in the fourth £1million transfer of his career, joining Manchester City, with 16 league goals in 53 appearances, mostly as a substitute. As injuries began to curtail game time, he had four months with Chelsea (7 league goals in 16 appearances). In March 1992 he moved to West Ham United, where he scored 17 league goals in 38 appearances with a vital goal on the final day of the 1992/93 season versus Cambridge United to see Billy Bonds' side go up to the Premier League on goal difference. He then had brief spells with his seventh London club, Millwall, and 'up North' with Carlisle United.

Clive Allen: English league record – 181 league goals in 388 league appearances. 243 career club goals.

In 1997 he had a stint as an NFL kicker for the London Monarchs. He was also one of the original pundits on *Soccer Saturday* with Jeff Stelling on Sky Sports.

He served Spurs as Development Coach and Assistant First Team Coach, most notably alongside Harry Redknapp.

In May 2017 he was part of a parade of club legends at Spurs' final home game at White Hart Lane. A salute for a goalscoring great! With an embrace from fellow former Spurs players, dad Les and cousin Paul, some things are even more important than football.

Allan Clarke

As the Leeds United centre forward for a decade, Allan 'Sniffer' Clarke was one of the greatest and best known goalscorers of his generation.

One of five footballing brothers, as a schoolboy supporter he would go behind the goal at Molineux or The Hawthorns and watch the strikers. "Then I would catch the bus back home to Short Heath and would be straight out on the council football pitch, practising what I had seen. My mum could watch us from the kitchen window, we lived and breathed on them."

A Black Country lad, he played for South Staff Boys and was called 'Tiny Clarke'. Picked up as a trainee for Walsall, he turned professional by seventeen in 1963, and had shot up to six foot by the time he was nineteen.

With the Saddlers he scored 41 league goals in 72 Third Division appearances. In March 1966 he was signed by First Division Fulham for £37,500. 45 goals in 85 top-flight appearances followed, but neither Allan Clarke's goals nor the legendary Johnny Haynes could keep Fulham up and they were relegated in the 1967/68 season.

Leicester City moved in and signed Clarke for a British record fee of £150,000 in June 1968. In the 1969 FA Cup Final semi-final he scored the only goal of the game versus West Brom (the club he supported as a boy).

In the Wembley final, he was voted Man of the Match despite Leicester losing one-nil to Manchester City. Clarke scored 12 league goals in 36 appearances and suffered another relegation as the Foxes lost their First Division status.

In the summer he made another record-breaking move, this time to Leeds United for £165,000. A few days after his 23rd birthday he made his debut for Don Revie's League Champions in the Charity Shield victory over City at Elland Road.

A month later he scored twice as Leeds recorded their biggest win, 10-0 versus Lyn Oslo in the 1st Round of the European Cup. Chasing a treble, Clarke was Leeds' top scorer with 26 goals. Reaching the semi-finals in Europe, they were defeated by Celtic, where in the second leg at Hampden Park a UEFA competition record crowd of 136,505 were in attendance. In the league they finished runners-up to Everton and after a replay at Old Trafford lost the FA Cup Final to Chelsea.

In season 1970/71 Leeds were runners-up in the league, with Clarke scoring all four goals versus Burnley in April 1971, and won the final of the Fairs Cup, the forerunner to the UEFA Cup. The first leg in Turin versus Juventus (Bettega, Causio et al) had to be abandoned due to heavy rain and a waterlogged pitch.

The re-arranged match in Italy finished 2-2 and in the second leg at Elland Road, Clarke's goal in a 1-1 draw was decisive to give Leeds their first European trophy.

In 1971/72, going for the double, in the Centenary FA Cup Final Leeds clashed with Arsenal. From a Mick Jones cross, Sniffer Clarke scored a wonderful diving header to win the game. Leeds were denied the league by Derby County, but Allan Clarke's only goal of the game had won Leeds United the cup for the first time in club history and a second cup final man of the match award.

The following season, Clarke scored the only goal over both semi-final legs versus Hajduk Split in the European Cup Winners' Cup. Unfortunately, over the space of twelve days, Leeds lost two cup finals. Shocked by Second Division Sunderland in the FA Cup final at Wembley and defeated by AC Milan in their European final in Greece, on both occasions by a single goal.

Fighting back the next season, Leeds set a new record of 29 league matches unbeaten from the start of a league campaign, ending the 1973/74 season as Champions of England with Clarke's goal in a 3-2 victory versus Ipswich Town at Elland Road clinching the title and giving him his first Championship winners medal.

In season 1974/75, now under the management of Jimmy Armfield, Leeds mixed it with the best in Europe. Clarke, along with captain Billy Bremner, scored in a 2-1 home victory over a Barcelona side containing Cruyff and Neeskens to win through on aggregate. In the final in Paris they tackled holders Bayern Munich. Refereeing decisions went again Leeds – Peter Lorimer had a goal disallowed and Clarke had a penalty claim waved away after a foul by Beckenbauer. It was not to be their night and the great Gerd Muller retained the European Cup for Bayern.

It was to be his final hurrah as injuries restricted his appearances and an ageing side broke up. On the big stage one more time, he scored in the FA Cup semi-final defeat to Manchester United in 1977.

By the end of the 1977/78 season, Clarke had played his final match for Leeds United. 110 league goals in 273 league appearances, 151 goals in total.

As a Leeds player he won 19 England caps, including under Revie, scoring 10 international goals. He found the net on his debut in World

Cup Mexico 1970 versus Czechoslovakia from the penalty spot. He also scored in the infamous Wembley 1-1 draw versus Poland and keeper Jan 'The Clown' Tomaszewski in a World Cup qualifier in October 1973, a result which ultimately cost England qualification and Alf Ramsey his job. A month earlier he scored twice versus Austria in a 7-0 friendly win at Wembley. Earlier in the year on Saint Valentine's Day, to help celebrate the centenary of the Scottish FA, he hit a double at Hampden Park in a 5-0 England victory. In 1967, Clarke had also represented Young England versus the England senior team in the then annual pre-cup final game, where he scored twice along with Rodney Marsh in a 5-0 win at Highbury.

After Leeds, he stayed in Yorkshire as player/manager of Barnsley, leading the club to promotion to the Third Division in his first season in charge. At Oakwell he scored 15 league goals in 47 appearances for a grand total of 223 league goals in 513 league appearances.

Just after he had hung up his boots, he returned to Elland Road as manager. Given a mighty Leeds welcome, sadly he could not restore former glories and resigned after the club were relegated in 1981/82. He also managed Scunthorpe to promotion to the Third Division, Barnsley again and Lincoln City.

A clever, fast-moving centre forward, good with his head, he was part of an iconic side who had their names on the back of their walk out tops. Described by some as 'Dirty Leeds' because of the aggressive nature of their play, on their day they could play any side off the park, best illustrated in March 1972 with their famous 39 passes move versus Southampton at Elland Road, Allan 'Sniffer' Clarke, who give the 'Mighty Leeds' their goalscoring edge, scoring twice in a 7-0 victory.

Tony Cottee

Over the past 50 years, Tony Cottee is among a select band of footballers to have 200 or more league goals in the top flight of English Football. Ian Rush, Alan Shearer and Wayne Rooney complete the group.

On the all-time list since 1888 he is 17th, with many of the positions taken by players from the golden age of goalscoring in the 1920s and

1930s. Post-war he is the 6th highest goalscorer, with 214 top-flight goals, just ahead of Geoff Hurst, and in the company of Jimmy Greaves, Shearer, Nat Lofthouse, Rush and David Herd. 136 First Division goals, 78 Premier League goals. In an era where goalscorers are defined by their inclusion in the Premier League 100 goal club, his goalscoring legacy is sometimes overlooked.

Cottee himself admitted he "was obsessed with goals". Dating back to his primary school days he had kept scrapbook cuttings and can recall "almost every goal".

A lifelong West Ham United fan who 'bleeds Claret and Blue', Cottee attended matches at the Boleyn Ground as often as he found the net for the Hammers' juniors and youth teams, which was a lot! He then played for the reserves and was encouraged by manager John Lyall to "just keep scoring".

On New Year's Day 1983 he realised a dream, making his first-team debut aged 17 at home to Tottenham Hotspur. On 25 minutes, as the ball hit the bar, he instinctively did what he had always been urged to do by his dad: "Follow up, follow up." He raced past Steve Perryman and headed home the rebound. TC's first professional goal for his scrapbook collection.

Cottee was now part of an experienced first-team set up that included Alvin Martin, Trevor Brooking, Alan Devonshire and Ray Stewart. In October 1983, player and club created history. In the League Cup he scored his first senior hat-trick (a four-goal blitz) in a club record 10-0 victory versus Bury.

In 1985/86, in partnership with new signing Frank McAvennie, Cottee hit 26 goals, 20 in the league that saw West Ham achieve their highest ever league position of third in the First Division. Right up to the final game of the season, where Tony scored in a 3-2 win at West Brom, the Hammers challenged for the title, but were pipped by Merseyside giants, Liverpool and Everton. He was voted PFA Young Player of the Year.

In September 1986, he was awarded his first England cap away to Sweden in Stockholm. In total he represented his country seven times (all under Bobby Robson), six times as a late substitute without scoring.

In the 1986/87 season he struck a personal best 22 league goals, including hat-tricks away to QPR 3-2 and Coventry City 3-1 – crucial strikes as West Ham battled relegation until Easter.

In November 1987 he scored his best ever top flight goal, a

spectacular acrobatic volley versus Nottingham Forest.

After agonising over a move away from East London he chose Everton over Arsenal in a British record transfer of £2 million.

On his league debut at Goodison Park in August 1988 he scored a hat-trick, the first goal after 34 seconds in a 4-0 win over Newcastle United. In his first season on Merseyside, he experienced two trips to Wembley. He scored twice in the final of the Full Members' Cup in a 4-3 defeat to Forest and three weeks later in the FA Cup Final, lost again this time to Liverpool 3-2.

In February 1991 Cottee was involved in one of the most famous cup ties and Merseyside derbies of all time. He scored twice, the 3rd and 4th goal equalisers in a 5th Round FA Cup replay versus Liverpool at Goodison Park that finished 4-4.

In his final season with Everton under his third manager, Mike Walker, following Colin Harvey and Howard Kendall, Cottee's goals went a long way to ensuring the Blues kept their Premier League status, surviving relegation on the final day of the 1993/94 season.

Two months earlier, in March 1994, Cottee had played for a Premier League XI in the Bobby Moore Memorial Match at Upton Park, scoring in a 2-1 win to mark the opening of the new stand in honour of the great man. This seemed to pave the way for a return to West Ham. After 99 goals in 241 league and cup games for Everton he was on his way back to East London as part of an exchange deal with David Burrows.

Re-joining at the start of the 1994/95 season under Harry Redknapp he hit a further 30 goals in two seasons, including the club's first hat-trick in the Premier League, in December 1994 in a 3-0 victory versus Manchester City at Upton Park, one of thirteen hat-tricks in his English club career. In total, Cottee over two spells scored 115 league goals in 256 appearances for West Ham United, 146 goals in total.

There followed a year in Malaysia with Selangor FC where he won a cup with 13 goals in 24 appearances.

Aged 32, he returned to English football in 1997 with Leicester City. Under Martin O'Neill he scored 34 goals in 100 appearances, most notably notching all three of Leicester's semi-final goals versus Sunderland in the 1999 League Cup. The final was lost against Spurs but in the year 2000, victory over Tranmere Rovers at Wembley ensured that Tony won his first winners medal in English football.

Cottee also had spells with Birmingham City, Norwich City,

player/manager with Barnet, before his final club call with Millwall up to the end of the 2000/2001 season.

In 2018 he was asked to play himself in the film *Score* (the director was a West Ham fan).

In 2019 he survived a brain haemorrhage with the help and quick thinking of friend and fellow Sky Sports pundit Phil Thompson. “I will forever be thankful to Thommo.”

Growing up, his role model had been West Ham forward, Bryan ‘Pop’ Robson. “I remember when ‘Pop’ got to 200 league goals and thinking, how fantastic, that became my target.” For the record and scrapbook memories collection: 115 West Ham, 72 Everton, 27 Leicester, 1 Birmingham City, 2 Norwich City and 9 Barnet. Tony Cottee: 226 English league goals, 214 in the top flight!

Kenny Dalglish

The most decorated goalscorer in the history of British football. A medals collection that runneth over with silverware. King Kenny won three European Cups and every domestic honour going in Scotland and England.

An outstanding individual talent who was always a team player. If it is questioned that he was an out and out goalscorer, 339 career club goals for Celtic and Liverpool confirm his goalscoring credentials.

It is just he was so good at everything else, bringing team mates into the game, as commentator Alan Parry said, "The creator supreme." The ultimate Fantasy Football player: 230 top-flight goals with 150 in championship winning seasons, with as many assists again!

Kenneth Mathieson Dalglish was born in Dalmarnock, East Glasgow and grew up a Rangers supporter. After leaving school he worked in various jobs, in a warehouse, a van-boy and as an apprentice joiner.

Playing for Glasgow United he was scouted by Liverpool and, aged 15 in August 1966, was invited for a trial. Meeting Bill Shankly, he played for the 'B team' versus Southport at Melwood. Shanks was keen to take the youthful Dalglish, but along with his parents, Kenny felt he was too young to leave home. He also had a trial with Ron Greenwood's West Ham United.

The following year Kenny was signed up by Jock Stein and assistant manager Sean Fallon for Celtic FC. Just sixteen, he was farmed out to Celtic nursery side Cumbernauld United. He then graduated to the reserves 'The Quality Street Gang', more often than not playing in midfield. He made his league debut against Raith Rovers in October 1969.

Aged 20, he established himself in the first team during the 1971/72 season. Now operating more as a striker, he scored his first derby league goal in the Old Firm match in a 3-2 win over Rangers at Ibrox in September 1971 (Dalglish had been in attendance in January 1971 at the Ibrox Stadium tragedy). By the end of the season, he had won his first honours with a league and Scottish Cup double.

In the 1972/73 season Dalglish hit a personal high 41 goals in 53 games as Celtic retained the title. A third consecutive championship was secured in 1973/74 (giving the club a record nine league titles in a row) along with another Scottish Cup triumph. In 1974/75 the Scottish Cup and League Cup were won.

Newly appointed captain for the 1975/76 season, Celtic did not win a trophy, but Dalglish was the Scottish Premier league top scorer with 24 league goals, 32 in total.

In Europe, twice Celtic reached the semi-finals of the European Cup. In 1971/72, after two goalless draws versus Inter Milan, at the end of the second leg before 75,000 at Parkhead, Celtic lost 5-4 on penalties. In 1973/74, Dalglish had scored in both legs of the quarter-final tie versus Basel but lost 2-0 on aggregate to Atletico Madrid in the semi-finals.

By the time Dalglish had won a third league and Scottish Cup double in 1976/77, he was seeking a move away after 112 league goals in 204 appearances, 167 goals in total. In August 1977 Celtic accepted Liverpool's British record offer of £440,000 and he returned to Merseyside, eleven years after his initial trial, this time as a replacement for Kevin Keegan who was on his way to Germany with SV Hamburg.

Dalglish scored on his league debut for Bob Paisley's side away to Middlesbrough and by the end of the season had 31 goals, with 20 in the league. The Reds were runners-up in the league and League Cup, denied both times by Brian Clough's Nottingham Forest.

In Europe, in December 1977 Dalglish scored in the Anfield leg of the European Super Cup Final in a 6-0 victory over Kevin Keegan's Hamburg. In the semi-final of the European Cup, he scored the Reds' second in a 3-0 return leg victory at Anfield over old rivals Borussia Moenchengladbach. In the final at Wembley, versus FC Bruges, Kenny, receiving a pass from Graeme Souness, chipped the ball over the keeper for the only goal of the game, as Liverpool were once again Champions of Europe.

In September 1978 Dalglish scored twice in the Anfield sunshine versus Tottenham Hotspur in a glorious 7-0 victory. He hit 21 league goals as the title was won and retained in 1979/80.

After three ever present league seasons, Dalglish missed games through injury in 1980/81, with the Reds finishing fifth in his absence. The League Cup was won for the first time in club history, with Kenny scoring seven, including in the semi-final leg at Anfield versus Manchester City and in the final victory over West Ham in a Villa Park replay. A third European Cup was secured with a one-nil win versus Real Madrid.

In seasons 1981/82 and 1982/83, the league and League Cup were both won, with Dalglish scoring at the Kop End against old team mate Ray Clemence in May 1982 versus Spurs to secure the Reds the title in a 3-1 win. By now it was a familiar sight for the three jocks, Dalglish, Hansen and Souness to be photographed together after a trophy triumph.

Under new manager Joe Fagan, the league, European Cup and League cup were won in 1983/84. On 29th May 1985, the events before the European Cup Final versus Juventus at the Heysel Stadium in Brussels overshadowed everything and Liverpool, along with all English clubs, were banned from European competition.

With Joe Fagan retiring as manager, Dalglish was offered the post of player/manager, aged 34. Assisted by 'boot room boys' Ronnie Moran and Roy Evans, he accepted on the condition that Bob Paisley could be by his side for the first season or so.

In the 1985/86 season, Dalglish played himself sparingly as Everton led the league. He returned himself to the starting line-up and the Reds won 11 of their final 12 league games, Dalglish's goal versus Chelsea at Stamford Bridge on the final day of the league season winning the Championship. A week later the fairy tale was complete by beating Everton in the FA Cup Final with the player/manager on the Wembley 'Anfield South' pitch.

Dalglish made a substitute appearance in the 1987 League Cup Final defeat to Arsenal and the Reds were runners-up to Everton in the league. Now a full-time manager, the league was won again in 1987/88 and, just weeks after the Hillsborough Disaster, an emotionally charged FA Cup Final was won versus Everton in May 1989.

In May 1990 he made his final appearance in a red shirt as Liverpool were presented with league title number 18 after the match at Anfield versus Derby. He had scored 118 league goals in 355 league appearances with 172 goals in total and was voted Footballer of the Year in 1978/79 and 1982/83.

On Friday 22nd February 1991, two days after the 4-4 FA Cup replay with Everton at Goodison Park, Dalglish shocked the world of football by resigning as manager of Liverpool Football Club, citing the pressure and the affect upon his health. Dalglish had left Liverpool, where he had found the club, at the top of the league.

In October 1991 he returned to the game as manager of Blackburn Rovers, leading the club to promotion and to the Premier League title, winning the championship on the final day of the 1994/95 season at Anfield.

He also managed Newcastle United and Celtic to the League Cup in 2000. In January 2011, he returned as manager of Liverpool and won the

League Cup in 2012 at the new Wembley on penalties versus Cardiff City.

For Scotland, Dalglish won a record 102 international caps, with a shared record of 30 goals. He played at three World Cups: 1974, 1978, scoring versus Holland, and 1982, finding the net against New Zealand. Memorable moments included winners versus England at both Hampden Park and Wembley, a header at Anfield versus Wales in 1977 to ensure World Cup qualification, two Kenny specials away to Belgium in 1982 and in 1984 a trademark goal versus Spain at Hampden to equal Denis Law's international goals record.

In 2017, the Centenary Stand at Anfield was renamed the Kenny Dalglish Stand, with 'Sir' added the following year after Kenny was honoured with a knighthood. In 2020, Dalglish, as director was on hand at the presentation for the Reds' nineteenth top-flight title on the Kop alongside manager Jurgen Klopp and captain Jordan Henderson as the Reds won the Premier League.

Ball at his feet, back to goal, with the ability to turn on a sixpence, Dalglish is the only player to have scored 100 league goals in Scotland and England with two single clubs. Above all the footballing accolades with Celtic, Liverpool and Scotland, Kenny, along with his wife Marina are recognised by the people on Merseyside following the Hillsborough Disaster for always 'being there'. Seeing the Kop covered in flowers, scarves and tributes he said, "It was the saddest and most beautiful sight I had ever seen."

Kerry Dixon

Uniquely in the history of English football, Kerry Dixon is the top scorer for three consecutive seasons in three separate divisions of the Football League: 1982/83 Third Division, 1983/84 Second Division and 1984/85 First Division. A feat even more impressive considering each subsequent season he ascended the league ladder to a higher division, reaching the pinnacle in the top flight.

This was a lesson in endeavouring to persevere. Dixon had suffered setbacks as a teenager. At Luton Town, he was not offered an apprenticeship and after featuring for the Tottenham Hotspur youth team and reserves, he was released without playing for the first team.

Born a free kick away from Kenilworth Road, as a youngster on match days he watched Luton's star striker Malcolm MacDonald.

Dixon himself had goals in him, once hitting 13 for Lewsey Centre in the Chiltern League. After his early disappointments he played non-league football for Chesham United and Dunstable Town.

Third Division Reading offered him the opportunity of league football. With his previous knock backs, he reached an amicable arrangement with manager Maurice Evans, whereby he would join on a part-time basis whilst completing his engineering studies.

A month after his 19th birthday in August 1980, he scored his first league goal in 2-1 away win at Griffin Park versus Brentford.

In the 1982/83 season he was the Third Division top scorer with 26 league goals, including a four-goal haul in a 7-5 defeat to Doncaster Rovers in September 1982. Even allowing for his goals, Reading were relegated.

Chelsea put in a bid and after 51 league goals in 116 appearances he left Elm Park for Stamford Bridge, proving to be a bargain £175,000. Manager John Neal played Dixon from the start, scoring twice on his league debut in a 5-0 win over Derby County on the opening day of the 1983/84 season.

It was the shape of things to come, as Dixon struck up a partnership with David Speedie, aided by winger Pat Nevin. Again, he was top scorer with 28 league goals, most memorably with a hat-trick at home to Leeds United as Chelsea won the Second Division Championship to return to the top flight.

In Dixon's first season in the First Division, he again scored on the opening day in August 1984, with a stunning volley versus Arsenal in the Highbury sunshine to earn Chelsea a 1-1 draw.

In November he hit two hat-tricks, first in the league in a 6-2 victory over Coventry City and then in the League Cup with a treble versus Manchester City in a 4-1 win. In total he scored eight League Cup goals as Chelsea reached the semi-finals, but disappointingly lost both legs to Sunderland.

Back to the league again, Kerry struck gold, finishing the season as the leading First Division goalscorer, shared with Gary Lineker on 24 league goals, with Chelsea finishing in a creditable sixth place.

70 goals for the Blues in 101 appearances over two seasons caught the eye of the England Manager, Bobby Robson. Dixon was included in the squad for the Azteca 2000 Tournament and featured in three games.

In June 1985 he made his international debut as a late substitute versus Mexico. On his full debut versus West Germany, he scored twice in a 3-0 win. "As a debut it was one of the great days of my life, playing for England was every kid's dream, on the Panini stickers, it was Kerry Dixon, Chelsea and England." Four days later he hit another brace in a 5-0 win over the USA in Los Angeles. He also appeared in the 1986 World Cup Finals versus Poland. Kerry Dixon, Chelsea and England: 8 caps 4 goals.

In season 1985/86 Dixon scored both Chelsea goals in a 2-1 win at Old Trafford versus Manchester United, but a muscle injury in the new year ruled him out of the Full Members' Final as manager John Hollins guided the Blues to a 5-4 victory over Manchester City.

After a play-off defeat to Middlesbrough, Chelsea were relegated in 1987/88. Kerry scored 25 league goals as Chelsea returned as Second Division champions with a record points tally of 99. In 1989/90, Dixon scored 20 more top-flight goals including a final day hat-trick away to Millwall to earn Chelsea, under Bobby Campbell, a fifth place finish, their highest in the league since the Osgood and Harris side of 1969/70.

Over the next two seasons, Dixon closed in on the club record scorer Bobby Tambling's 202 goals, but after the muscle injury he was never the same player. In 1992, just nine goals short of the Chelsea record, 193 goals with 147 league goals in 335 league appearances, he was sold to Southampton for £575,000. With the Saints he scored twice in 9 league appearances.

In February 1993 he joined home club Luton, scoring 19 league goals in 75 appearances. In an FA Cup run in 1994, Dixon played versus Chelsea in the Wembley semi-final defeat.

He then had brief spells with Millwall (9 league goals in 31 appearances) and Watford (no goals from 11 league appearances).

As player/manager of Doncaster Rovers (3 league goals in 16 appearances) he steered the club safely away from relegation in the 1996/97 season.

After league football, he returned to the non-league game as a player and later in management, back with Dunstable Town. Dixon's personal issues with gambling and drugs, his time in prison and subsequent work as a heating engineer's assistant are well documented, not least in his autobiography *Up Front*.

He has also been involved with Chelsea FC match day hospitality and a football school in his home community in Dunstable.

Kerry Dixon – a true blue, Chelsea legend. Career figures with seven clubs of 231 league goals in 593 league appearances.

After playing for Luton versus Chelsea in the 1994 Wembley FA Cup semi-final he recalled, "That was one of the greatest days of my life in football, we lost 2-0, but afterwards it seemed the whole ground was singing my name."

Bob Latchford

At the highest level in English league football, Bob Latchford was the most prolific goalscorer of his time. For a decade, from the early 1970s to the early 1980s, he scored more top-flight goals than anyone.

For the eleven consecutive First Division seasons from 1972/73 to 1982/83 inclusive he recorded 167 league goals for Birmingham City, Everton and Swansea City.

He added a further two for Coventry City, giving him 169 top-flight league goals. Over the course of his Football League career, he scored 218 English league goals, plus 13 in the Dutch league for a grand total of 231 league goals in 545 appearances. For the record, in 1981, Latchford also scored 4 in 4 for Brisbane Lions in the National Soccer League in Australia.

Latchford grew up in King's Heath in the south of Birmingham, playing in the back garden with his brothers Peter and Dave, both of whom would play professionally as goalkeepers with Celtic and Birmingham City respectively.

Playing for South Birmingham Boys and Warwickshire County Schools, Latchford was offered an apprenticeship by Birmingham City Football Club. Aged eighteen, he scored twice on his league debut at St. Andrews in March 1969 versus Preston North End.

Under the management of Freddie Goodwin, he formed a front three with Trevor Francis and Bob Hatton. In the 1971/72 season, playing in the famous blue and white penguin strip, Latchford was the Second Division top scorer with 23 league goals with a last day winner at Orient clinching promotion to the First Division. Birmingham also reached the semi-finals of the FA Cup, defeated by Leeds United.

In August 1972 he played in the match that was involved in the very first penalty shoot-out in FA Cup history, beating Stoke City 4-3 on spot kicks in the third-place play-off match (at the time in operation for defeated semi-finalists). Geoff Hurst scored for Stoke in the shoot-out. In his first season in the top flight, he scored 19 league goals as Birmingham finished in mid table. In February 1974, with 68 league goals in 160 appearances for City, Latchford was transferred to Everton for a British record fee of £350,000 with Howard Kendall and Archie Styles part of the exchange deal.

In season 1974/75, under the management of Billy Bingham, Everton challenged for the league title. In January 1975, probably uniquely, Bob scored twice versus his brother Dave in a 3-0 win over Birmingham at St. Andrews. Everton, who had led the league, finished fourth, only three points behind champions Derby County with Bob saying, "The 74/75 championship was the one we should have won."

In the 1976/77 season Everton were unfortunate to lose a controversial FA Cup semi-final replay to Liverpool. In the League Cup, a classic Bob Latchford header saw off Bolton in the semi-final. In the final versus Aston Villa, after a Wembley stalemate, he scored in both replays at Hillsborough and Old Trafford, but again was denied silverware as Villa won 3-2 after extra time.

In 1977/78, Latchford was the first Everton player to be the leading goalscorer in the English top flight since Tommy Lawton did so in successive seasons some forty years earlier in the late 1930s. Everton finished third in the league under Gordon Lee and Latchford was the number one goalscorer in the country. In October '77 he hit a hat-trick versus QPR in a 5-1 win, which included assists from the regular supply line of Andy King and Dave Thomas. The following month, Coventry were hit for six with another Latchford hat-trick.

On 29 April 1978, exactly 45 years to the day since Everton's original Number 9, Dixie Dean, had scored in the FA Cup Final of 1933, Bob scored twice past Peter Bonetti in a 6-0 triumph over Chelsea at Goodison Park to take his tally for the season to 30 league goals. Latchford was carried shoulder high on the pitch with Evertonians singing "Bobby Latchford walks on water". The £10,000 prize he won, put up by the Daily Express if anyone in the First Division reached 30 league goals, he generously shared with team mates, ground staff and charities. After the match he was congratulated by Dixie, shaking hands, "Well done lad, 30 goals, great achievement."

In 1980 Latchford scored in the FA Cup semi-final replay at Elland Road, but Everton lost out as West Ham headed to Wembley. With Everton, he scored 106 league goals in 236 appearances with 138 goals in total.

In the summer of 1981, he moved to newly-promoted Swansea City, managed by John Toshack, whom Latchford had many a tussle with on Merseyside derby day. In August 1981 he scored a hat-trick in the Swans' first league match in the top flight, in a 5-1 win at the Vetch Field versus Leeds. Finishing a very creditable sixth place, Swansea were relegated the following season. Latchford won two Welsh Cups and departed midway through the 1983/84 season with 35 league goals from 87 appearances.

He joined NAC Breda in Holland, helping gain promotion to the top division with 13 league goals in 15 appearances. He returned to England in the First Division with Coventry, netting 2 league goals in 12 appearances. He then had spells with Lincoln City (2 league goals in 15 games) and Newport County (5 league goals in 20 games). He also won another Welsh Cup in 1987 with non-league Merthyr Tydfil.

At international level he won twelve caps, scoring five goals. He made his international debut in England's 2-0 World Cup qualifying victory against Italy in November 1977 at Wembley. He opened his account versus Wales in May 1978 at Ninian Park, Cardiff. In a European Championship qualifier versus Northern Ireland in February 1979 he scored twice. England qualified for Euro '80 and although Bob Latchford, Everton and England, was featured in the Europa '80 sticker album No.126 he did not play in the championships. In another sticker collection Panini '83, No. 291, he is pictured smiling in his socks in

Swansea kit.

After his playing days, Latchford was involved in sports agency and marketing. He was also part of the Youth Academy at Birmingham City under old team mate Trevor Francis. He moved to live in Austria and now resides in Germany.

In 2001 he received the Dixie Dean Memorial Award for his footballing contribution on Merseyside. In 2006, his autobiography *A Different Road* helped raise money for the EFPF, a fan run benevolent fund for former Everton players who had fallen on hard times.

Bob said, "Evertonians are so enthusiastic about their players, it staggers me every time I come over. I might have started at Birmingham, but my soul is at Goodison."

Gary Lineker

Sometimes even the greatest of goalscorers need their lucky boots as Gary Lineker explained to Danny Baker on their podcast *Lineker and Baker: Behind Closed Doors*.

Lineker said, "I had a pair of lucky boots, I couldn't stop scoring, it was like a goal a game building up to the World Cup in 1986. I was knocking them in for fun. I was at Everton and we were top of the league." The boots went missing and Lineker, wearing a replacement pair, missed a couple of chances as Everton lost a crucial game at Oxford that ultimately cost them the title.

"I got my boots back for the next game and scored a hat-trick against Southampton and two in the last match with West Ham to finish with 30 league goals for the season. They were now absolutely knackered these boots with holes in them and everything, so I sent them to Adidas and they fixed them for me for the World Cup. They patched them together and I won the Golden Boot. Even during the World Cup they fell apart again but we had them sent off and specially repaired again and they are now in the Adidas Museum in Germany."

It had only been four seasons earlier that the World Cup top scorer had been trying to establish himself in the first team with his home town club Leicester City. Coming through the youth ranks, Lineker's boyhood hero was the Foxes' centre-forward Frank Worthington. As a child and then a young player he would help out on the family fruit and vegetable market stall in Leicester.

He was given his league debut by Jock Wallace on New Year's Day 1979 versus Oldham at Filbert Street, just over a month after his eighteen birthday. In April he scored his first league goal in a 1-0 away win at Meadow Lane versus Notts County. Naturally pacey, he was played on the right wing and was part of the squad that won the Second Division championship in 1979/80 and were then relegated the following season.

He made his breakthrough in season 1981/82, playing more regularly through the middle, scoring 17 league goals. Leicester reached the semi-finals of the FA Cup with the match at Villa Park against Tottenham, delayed by a cockerel (Spurs' symbol) on the pitch but was defeated two-nil on the day.

In 1982/83, under Gordon Milne, Lineker was the Second Division top scorer, winning the Silver Boot with 26 league goals, winning promotion back to the top flight. In 1984/85 he is again top scorer, this time in the First Division with a Golden Boot shared with Kerry Dixon with 24 league goals, including a hat-trick versus Aston Villa in a 5-0 win in October 1984. In the summer of 1985, Lineker was signed for £800,000 by champions Everton, as a replacement for Andy Gray. With Leicester City FC he scored 95 league goals in 194 league appearances.

Playing up front with Graeme Sharp, Howard Kendall's side had a midfield quartet of Bracewell, Reid, Sheedy and Steven. Lineker's goals won over the Goodison faithful after the departure of their favourite forward. Their new Number 8 scored 30 in the league, including three hat-tricks, Birmingham City (4-1), Manchester City (4-0) and Southampton (6-1), and in both Merseyside derbies as the First Division top scorer for 1985/86 season. He was the first goalscorer to be the top scorer in successive seasons in the top flight since Ron Davies of Southampton in the late 1960s. Everton finished runners-up in the league and although Lineker scored the opening goal in the FA Cup Final, the match was lost to Liverpool.

Lineker's goals won him another Golden Boot and the Footballer of the Year and PFA Player of the Year awards. Forty goals in all competitions: League 30, FA Cup 5, League Cup 3 and Screen Sport Super Cup 2.

After the Mexico '86 World Cup he moved to Barcelona, signing for Terry Venables for £2.75m. In three seasons at the Nou Camp he had three coaches. In his first season under El Tel, he scored on his Barca league debut versus Racing Santander and in January 1987 hit a hat-trick versus Real Madrid, finishing the season as runners-up in La Liga. In 1987/88, under Luis Aragones, he scored in the second leg of the Spanish Cup semi-final versus Osasuna as Barca won the Copa del Rey. In his third and final season he was beset by niggling injuries and was played on the wing by Johan Cruyff. He scored in both legs of the semi-final of the European Cup Winners' Cup, with the Catalan giants winning the final versus Italian side Sampdoria. With Barca, 'El Matador' scored 42 goals in 103 La Liga appearances.

In 1989 Lineker returned to England, teaming up again with Venables, signing for Tottenham Hotspur for £1.1m. In three seasons at White Hart Lane he scored 67 league goals in 105 appearances. In his first season (1989/90) he was the First Division top scorer (with a record third different club) with 24 league goals including hat-tricks versus QPR and Norwich City as Spurs finished third in the league.

In 1990/91 he scored twice in the first ever FA Cup semi-final to be played at Wembley, with Spurs beating Arsenal 3-1. In the final he had a penalty saved by Nottingham Forest keeper Mark Crossley as Spurs won the cup with a one in the year.

In season 1991/92 he scored in both legs of the League Cup semi-final defeat by Forest. He scored 28 league goals, including a four-goal haul in an away day win at Wimbledon, 3-5. Lineker was also voted Footballer of the Year, the first player to win the award with two separate clubs. By the end of the 1991/92 season, he had scored 282 club goals in England and Spain including 234 league goals. After two years with Grampus Eight in the Japanese J League he retired from playing.

At international level he won 80 international caps with 48 goals. He is third on the all-time list of British international goalscorers. He captained his country eighteen times. His five hat-tricks (second only to Jimmy Greaves) include four goals at the Bernabeu versus Spain whilst a Barca player. He scored his first England goal whilst still a Leicester player in March 1985 versus the Republic of Ireland at Wembley. In the summer he scored twice versus the USA. A year later the world would know his name. He was the World Cup Golden Boot winner, top scorer with six goals at Mexico '86. A hat-trick (England's first at a World Cup Finals since Geoff Hurst in 1966) versus Poland in the final group match, a brace in the last 16 against Paraguay and one versus Argentina in the Maradona 'Hand of God' quarter-final 2-1 loss.

Four years later, in Italia '90, he scored four more – versus Ireland in the group stage and two penalties in the quarter-final 3-2 win over Cameroon. In the semi-final he scored versus Germany and also in the penalty shoot-out 4-3 loss. Lineker remarked, "Football is a simple game: twenty-two men chase a ball for 90 minutes, and at the end, the Germans always win." With ten World Cup Finals goals he is joint 8th on the leading World Cup scorers all-time list.

Throughout his playing years, Lineker was never booked or sent off. "As my career developed, this whole 'He's never had a yellow card' thing emerged. I wasn't a saint. Being in Spain for three years, where cards pop out all over the place, it was a miracle I didn't get one. People used to joke with me. 'Why don't you just punch the ref for a laugh?' which obviously would have been really stupid, but it might have been funny in my last game."

An all-round sportsman, he represented Leicestershire Schools at cricket and is more than useful at both golf and snooker. Lucky boots or not, a goal hanger with a collection of a Silver Boot and four Golden Boots, Gary Lineker, the goalscoring great with the ultimate goalden touch was as proud as punch as *Match of the Day* presenter as 'his club' Leicester City won the Premier League in 2015/16 and was emotionally delighted to be there in person to witness the FA Cup triumph at Wembley in 2021.

He remains the only player to be the top-flight leading goalscorer in the history of English football with three separate clubs: Leicester City, Everton and Tottenham Hotspur. Lineker was a strong opponent of the introduction of a European Super League and reminds supporters that there was a time when football existed before the Premier League.

Ted MacDougall

Mac the Nine! In his kaleidoscope playing days, Scottish international Edward John MacDougall was the leading aggregate goalscorer in English football with 308 career goals, including 256 league goals in 535 appearances.

He was a natural predatory goalscoring poacher. As a kid at Inverness Clachnacuddin ground, where his dad had been a goalkeeper, he recalled, "I remember my dad putting a slipper on my right foot to encourage me to kick with my left."

Just before his twelfth birthday, Ted and his mum and dad had to leave the Highlands as work on the railways dried up and the family moved to Lancashire where his mum had grown up.

Living in Widnes, after he left school at fifteen, he played in the amateur leagues and began an apprenticeship as a compositor with the local newspaper. While attending a print and design course at Liverpool College of Art, he would see The Beatles perform on a Monday night in Widnes, which was fab as Ted shares his birthday with Elvis.

His foreman at the local newspaper had contacts with Liverpool Football Club and helped arrange a trial with the Reds and he was taken on as a trainee. He made the substitute bench but never played for the first team. However, he has fond memories: "I have never lost my love for Liverpool, I still love the club and I loved the way I was brought up there."

Aged 20, MacDougall moved on to Fourth Division York City, where over two seasons, 1967-68 and 1968/69, he had three managers including Tom Lockie who had signed him. Ted recalls: "City had one match ball, it was re-painted after every game and used again for the next match before it became worn out and was then used for training."

He made a goalscoring debut versus Workington and, even with York struggling at the foot of the table, Ted scored 34 league goals in 84 appearances.

In 1969, MacDougall was signed for £10,000 by Freddie Cox, manager of Bournemouth & Boscombe Athletic FC (name changed in 1972 to AFC Bournemouth). In two spells at Dean Court, 1969-1972 and 1978-1980, Super Ted's magic numbers were 119 league goals in 198 appearances with 144 goals in total. Under manager John Bond he set league and cup goalscoring records.

In the league he was the leading goalscorer in English football for two consecutive seasons: 1970/71, scoring a club record 42 league goals as the Cherries won promotion from the Fourth Division, with MacDougall scoring 49 goals in all competitions, and 1971/72 – 35 league goals (shared with Alf Wood, Shrewsbury Town) with 47 goals in all competitions, finishing third in the Third Division but, unfortunately at the time, promotion to the Second Division was only in place for the top two, and was only introduced for the third place from the 1973/74 season.

In the FA Cup, after scoring a late equaliser at Oxford City in the 1st Round in November 1970, in the replay MacDougall struck a double hat-trick in an 8-1 victory. The following season at the same stage of the competition in November 1971 he scored NINE, setting an FA Cup individual scoring record in a club record 11-0 win versus Margate.

After his historic triple hat-trick, three days later he was invited to play in Geoff Hurst's testimonial match, MacDougall scoring for the European All-Stars team in a 4-4 draw at Upton Park.

In September 1972, Bournemouth accepted a club record £220,000 and he was transferred to Manchester United. "Denis Law was my hero and Georgie Best was the greatest ever. United were in transition and unfortunately I couldn't help them." Ted tried with 5 league goals in 18 appearances. He then moved onto West Ham United netting 5 league goals in 24 appearances. The highlight at both Uniteds were goals versus Liverpool.

In December 1973, he was again under the management of John Bond, this time at Norwich City. In the semi-final of the 1974/75 League Cup versus old club Manchester United, MacDougall's crucial away goal in a 2-2 draw at Old Trafford saw the Canaries through to Wembley. The final was with Aston Villa, the first time a major cup final was contested between two sides outside of the top flight, with Villa winning by a single goal.

In the league, his goals enabled City to return to the First Division. Back in the top flight he was an ever present alongside team mates Kevin Keelan and Martin Peters. He carried on scoring with 23 league goals, including hat-tricks versus Aston Villa and Everton and a third goal versus Liverpool, this time at Anfield. He became the First Division top marksman for season 1975/76 and the first ever Norwich City player to be leading goalscorer in the top flight of English football.

During his time in East Anglia he scored 51 league goals in 112 appearances.

While at Carrow Road, MacDougall also won all seven of his international caps for Scotland, scoring three times, finding the net on debut away to Sweden and at Hampden Park versus Northern Ireland and Denmark.

Joining Southampton, he played his first season of European football as the Saints reached the quarter-finals of the 1976/77 European Cup Winners' Cup. In the last eight tie, he scored along with a David Peach penalty in a famous 2-1 victory over holders Anderlecht, bowing out with a 3-2 aggregate loss.

At the Dell, he again linked up with Phil Boyer whom he had developed a partnership with at York City, Bournemouth and Norwich. He scored 42 league goals in 86 appearances and was involved in the third successful promotion campaign of his career as Lawrie

McMenemy's side finished runners up in the 1977/78 Second Division table to secure First Division football.

After MacDougall's second spell with Bournemouth, he completed his Football League career with Blackpool under Alan Ball whom he would also serve under as a scout with Portsmouth. He also played in Australia, South Africa, Canada and America.

He settled in the States, where he worked with GotFootball, involving youth football in the US. He also formed his own club! Atlanta Spurs FC.

In 2013 AFC Bournemouth renamed their South Stand in honour of their ace goalscorer. Now known as the Vitality Stadium, in his day there were few more vital goalscorers than Ted MacDougoal.

Malcolm MacDonald

On the front cover of the Playfair pocket *Football Annual* 1976/77, Malcolm MacDonald is in typical pose. Pictured in the colours of Newcastle United, running at full pelt, shoulder length hair flowing, sideburns showing, astride of Ipswich Town's John Wark.

Much to the dismay of all Newcastle fans, by the time the new season had begun their club had accepted a British record transfer fee and their favourite goalscoring Number 9 was on his way back to London to play in the red and white of Arsenal.

Some 20 years earlier he had been born in the capital in Fulham, and he lived just up the road from Craven Cottage. The family moved to East Sussex and MacDonald played at full-back for Tonbridge Angels, temporarily moved up front by manager Harry Haslam. Harry left to be chief scout at Fulham and on his recommendation manager Bobby Robson signed Malcolm for £1,000.

With a serious injury crisis among the forwards, Bobby played MacDonald up front permanently. In one season by the river, he scored 5 league goals in 13 appearances, and despite Fulham being relegated from the Second Division, Malcolm credited the boss: "Bobby was a great influence for me."

In July 1969 he joined Luton Town, managed by Alec Stock, for £17,500. In two seasons at Kenilworth Road, he scored 49 league goals in 88 appearances. In the 1969/70 season he hit 25 league goals, including a hat-trick in a 5-0 win versus Reading in March 1970 as the Hatters finished runners-up in the Third Division.

In the 1970/71 season in the Second Division, MacDonald grabbed another 24 league goals to send Luton to 6th place, their highest league position for a decade.

In May 1971, aged 21, he signed for Newcastle United and First Division football for £180,000. Three months later in August, the legend of Supermac began. Having predicted he would score a bagful of goals, on his home debut at St. James after none from the opening two games he struck a hat-trick in a 3-2 win over Liverpool. The supporters chanted to the tune of *Jesus Christ Superstar*, "Supermac, superstar, how many goals have you scored so far?" In his first season on Tyneside he topped 30 goals, two coming in the infamous FA Cup defeat to Hereford, one at home and one in the 2-1 replay defeat.

In the 1973/74 season he scored in every round of the FA Cup (7 goals) including the semi-final, with both goals versus Burnley in a 2-0 victory at Hillsborough. Before the final, Supermac was branded Supermouth after forecasting how he was going to do the same to Liverpool, but Emlyn Hughes and co held firm as the Geordies suffered a 3-0 loss in their first FA Cup Final since 1955.

In season 1974/75, as Newcastle United finished 15th in the league, MacDonald was the country's number one goalscorer as the First Division, the leading marksman with 21 league goals, including a couple versus Chelsea in a 5-0 win in November 1974.

In 1975/76 he scored 24 goals in league and cup. In partnership with Alan Gowling Newcastle reached the League cup Final for the first time in club history. In the final versus Manchester City there was further Wembley heartache with a 2-1 loss.

After five seasons he had 138 goals, with 95 league goals from 187 appearances and was in the same bracket of adoration as previous Newcastle United forwards in black and white such as Hughie Gallacher and Jackie Milburn.

Then, in the long hot summer of 1976, Newcastle supporters' hearts were broken when the club sold MacDonald for a new record British transfer fee of exactly a third of a million pounds. £333,333 and 34 pence!

Things could have worked out differently. Admired by Brian Clough at Nottingham Forest, Malcolm said, "I would have loved to play for Cloughie too. I was always left with the impression he saw himself in me. Like me, he was a goalscorer and finished early through injury. I had a brash attitude too, having that gave us an edge. But mine was for one reason, only to score goals."

As it was, Supermac joined Terry Neill's Arsenal in August 1976. In his first season he was First Division top scorer with 25 league goals (shared with Andy Gray), the highlight a hat-trick in a 5-3 win over Newcastle at Highbury in December 1976 when the gum chewing striker was applauded by both sets of fans at the final whistle.

In the 1977/78 season, again he scored in every round of the FA Cup leading up to the final, including another double in a semi-final in a 3-0 win versus Orient at Stamford Bridge. In the final MacDonald experienced a third Wembley cup final defeat, this time against old manager Bobby Robson's Ipswich Town.

In August 1978, in a League Cup tie away at Rotherham United, he caught his studs in the turf and felt his knee go, an injury that all but ended his football playing career at the age of 28 years old. He fought an uphill battle for ten months and did score in the final league game of the 1978/79 season versus Chelsea, just a couple of days after missing out on the FA Cup Final victory over Manchester United.

After going on loan to Djurgårdens in Sweden, scoring twice in nine appearances, he accepted his time was up. By the start of the 1979/80 season, MacDonald had 42 league goals in 84 appearances for Arsenal.

For England he scored six goals in 14 internationals under three managers, Alf Ramsey, Joe Mercer and Don Revie. In March 1975 he netted in a 2-0 Wembley win versus World Champions West Germany. A month later he scored a post-war record five goals versus Cyprus in a European Championship qualifier. The Wembley scoreboard read 'Supermac 5 Cyprus 0'. He also had a sixth goal disallowed!

As a manager, he returned to Fulham and led the club to the Second Division in 1982, and just missed out on the last day of the season on promotion to the First Division the following season. He also managed at Huddersfield Town.

Malcolm Macdonald, a modern-day throwback, to the days of Lofthouse and Lawton. As a youngster, in January 1951 at Craven Cottage he had witnessed Jackie Milburn play and score in a 5-4 Newcastle win over Fulham in the FA Cup. Like Jackie, Supermac was a sprinter – in 1975 he clocked an Olympic standard 10.4 seconds in the 100 metres in the BBC television *Superstars* series. He was though, very much his own man, his own goalscorer. In a decade of prolific forward play, he finished his career with 191 league goals in 372 appearances with 270 career goals.

Bryan 'Pop' Robson

When collecting football cards or stickers as a kid, sometimes certain footballers (like songs on the radio) would follow you around. Fortunately, one such was goalscorer Pop Robson, whom we had two

Topps football cards, one in the black and white stripes of Newcastle and one in West Ham claret and blue kit. We even had one in our Top Trumps 1979 (spelt Brian) in Hammers change strip just before Pop joined Sunderland.

Pop was not only popular with us, in the *Shoot!* Annual of 1984, Jimmy Greaves included Pop in his Top Ten goalscorers from his time in the game going back to 1957. Greavsie, a columnist with the magazine, said, "We played together when I was winding up my career at West Ham and he's a lovely fella. The greatest thing about Pop was his timing, his forward runs were perfectly judged and he was so quick he could even make one of my terrible passes look great."

If a player's popularity was to be gauged on their ability to return to their former clubs Pop Robson is surely among fans' favourites, having multiple spells with West Ham, Carlisle and Sunderland. Over 22 seasons from 1964/65 to 1985/86, covering 10 spells with five league clubs, Robson scored 265 league goals. Born on Armistice Day, since post-war league football resumed in the 1946/47 season, he is 14th on the all-time list of leading football league goalscorers.

Pop remembers: "I would go to Roker Park one week and St. James Park the next. It was always the same – play for the school in the morning, go to the match, have a pie and sit on the wall surrounding the pitch." Playing for local amateur side Clara Vale Juniors he was picked up by Newcastle United. He made his football league debut in season 1964/65 as Newcastle won the Second Division championship. Initially he was a speedy right winger, before being moved to central striker.

Robson credits his balance and nimble footwork to his mum and dad-in-law who were champion ballroom dancers who encouraged him to move on the balls of his feet, enabling him to move a yard or two quicker. He also played table tennis to county standard with his international playing wife Maureen, which helped with his agility.

Lightness of foot certainly paid off in season 1968/69. He scored in the league for Newcastle versus all his future clubs: West Ham United, Sunderland and Chelsea (Carlisle United were in a separate division).

In total Robson scored 30 goals in all competitions, with six in the European Fairs Cup. In partnership with Wyn Davies, Newcastle reached the final. Victories included overcoming Feyenoord, Sporting Lisbon and in the semi-final Glasgow Rangers. The two-legged final was won versus Ujpest Dozsa of Hungary 6-2 on aggregate. Joe Harvey's side remain the most recent Newcastle United team to win a major trophy.

The following season he scored 25 goals. In defence of their Fairs Cup, in Round Three versus Southampton, Robson and Saints' Mick Channon scored the only two goals of the tie, Pop's away goal proving decisive. In the quarter-final he scored twice against Anderlecht as Newcastle were knocked out on away goals. In the league he also scored a hat-trick in a 5-1 victory over Manchester United.

In 206 league games with Newcastle United he scored 82 league goals, 97 goals in total. The highest goal return in a single spell in his career and a legacy as the Geordies' favourite Mackem, as Pop had been born in Sunderland.

In February 1971 he moved for a club record £120,000 to London, joining West Ham, linking up with Greavsie and Geoff Hurst. In two spells with the Hammers (1971-74 and 1976-79) he scored 94 league goals in 227 appearances, 104 goals in total. In his first full season, 1971/72, he scored four goals in the League Cup as West Ham reached the semi-finals. The tie versus Stoke City turned into a seven-hour marathon over four matches (including two replays) with ultimately West Ham losing out. In the league, he also scored versus Newcastle at St. James Park in a 2-2 draw.

In 1972/73 he was a league ever present for a second consecutive season. Robson was the First Division top scorer with 28 league goals, the first West Ham player since Vic Watson in 1929/30 to be top-flight leading scorer. He also shared the title of overall top league marksman for the season with Fred Binney of Exeter City. West Ham finished in 6th place, the club's highest league position since 1958/59. Robson's goals included a hat-trick versus Southampton in a 4-3 win, a double versus Leicester in 5-2 victory and a goal against reigning champions Derby County. He also scored versus Liverpool, Manchester United, Spurs and Chelsea. Versus Manchester City both Robson and Ted MacDougall found the net in a 2-1 victory.

In his second spell with West Ham, he was Second Division top scorer with 24 league goals in season 1978/79 including a hat-trick versus Millwall. In between his two spells with West Ham, he joined Sunderland in July 1974 for £145,000, the first of three spells with his hometown club – 1974-76, 1979-81 and 1983/84 – scoring in total 60 league goals in 154 league appearances.

Twice his goals aided Sunderland's return to top flight football: In

1975/76 as Second Division champions and 1979/80 as runners-up, which was secured with a last day victory versus West Ham at Upton Park. In his third spell in 1983/84 (where he also had a brief spell as caretaker manager) he scored, aged 38½, in the last game of the season in a 2-0 win at Leicester City and Gary Lineker to guarantee Sunderland safety in the First Division.

In the 1980s, Robson also played for Chelsea in 1982/83 with 3 league goals in 15 appearances and he had three spells with Carlisle United which included a turn as player/coach, scoring 26 league goals in 72 appearances over seasons 1981/82, 1982/83 (on loan) and in his final two seasons of league football in 1984/85 and 1985/86. In 1981/82 he scored another vital last day goal, versus Chester City to seal promotion to the Second Division.

Robson represented the Football League and also England at Under 23 level, but never earned a full international appearance. "The best striker England never capped." – Jimmy Greaves. He was the first player to score for both sides in the Tyne-Wear derby. Moving around, Robson quipped that every time he left West Ham, the club won the FA Cup.

After his playing career he turned out in non-league for Gateshead and had further coaching/scouting roles with Hartlepool, Manchester United, Leeds United, Sunderland and Birmingham City. In 2020 Pop cut the ribbon to open a charity shop in support of Tynedale Hospice at Home. As a kid, you wished to have Robson's card in your Top Trumps hand. In his own childhood, along with two friends, he was given his nickname Pop after the Rice Krispies cereal characters Snap, Crackle and Pop!

Ian Rush

On a Tuesday in April 1987, the *Liverpool Echo* published Arrivederci Rushie! a souvenir special, farewell to a legend. By Saturday tea time as the Football Pink hit the streets, Rush had reached another milestone, the headline reading, "Rush equals Dixie Derby Record." Ian Rush struck twice versus Everton at Anfield before his summer move to Juventus to match Dixie Dean's Merseyside derby goals tally.

The Reds' goalscoring Number 9 was hailed as a modern day all-time great. "No one is in front of Rushie when it comes to goalscoring, Denis Law and Nat Lofthouse are probably level with him. Liverpool will never find anyone to replace him because he is the best in the world today." – Jimmy Greaves

"He would lurk on the shoulder of the last defender, Rushie moved, I passed, he scored, when one-on-one with the keeper, Rushie was utterly ruthless." – Kenny Dalglish.

Rush is lethal! 346 goals for Liverpool FC, a post-war best for a single English league club. 232 top-flight league goals, 4th on the post-war list and 14th on the all-time list in the history of English football.

His records include FA Cup (20th and 21st century) and League Cup record goalscorer with 43 and 49 goals respectively, most goals in FA Cup Finals 5, the first British player to win European Golden Boot, and a record 25 Merseyside derby goals. 411 career goals in total.

Born and brought up in North Wales from a family of ten brothers and sisters, along with mum and dad, Rushie had his own first team and substitute. As a child he was laid low with meningitis, but recovered to represent Deeside Schools and Wales schoolboys. As a youth he would go to watch Everton. "Bob Latchford was the only player I ever really idolised."

He was offered an apprenticeship by Third Division player/manager Alan Oakes at Chester City. In September 1979, a month short of his eighteenth birthday, he scored his first league goal away to Gillingham. After 14 league goals in 34 appearances plus a further 3 in the FA Cup, Liverpool offered Chester £300,000. Unsure whether to go, Oakes reassured Rushie that if things didn't work out he could always return to Chester.

After not scoring in 9 appearances, including in the 1981 League Cup Final replay and European Cup semi-final home leg, wise old owl Bob Paisley encouraged Rush to be more selfish in front of goal. His first Liverpool goal was versus Finnish side Oulu Palloseura in a European

Cup match at Anfield in September 1981. The following month he scored his first Liverpool league goals with two versus Allan Clarke's Leeds United at Anfield. In two spells over the next decade and a half he would score a club record 346 goals in 660 appearances: 229 league goals in 469 appearances, 39 FA Cup goals, 48 League Cup goals, 20 in Europe, 3 in the Charity Shield and 7 in the Screen Sport Super Cup.

In seasons 1981/82 and 1982/83 Rushie grabbed 30 and 31 goals as the Reds won both the league and League Cup. In the 1982 League Cup he scored in both semi-final legs versus Ipswich and also in the final versus Tottenham Hotspur.

In 1982/83 he was voted PFA Young Player of the Year after 24 league goals, including when in November 1982 he hit four in the league at Goodison versus Everton in a 5-0 away win.

In the 1983/84 season, he swept the board. First Division top scorer with 32 league goals as the Reds won a third successive league title – a Friday night hat-trick at Villa Park, at Anfield he scored four versus Coventry City and he hit Luton Town for five. He was the first British winner of the European Golden Boot since its inception in 1967/68 as the continent's leading league goalscorer. In the League Cup he scored 8 as the final was won in a replay at Maine Road versus Everton. In the European Cup, he scored twice in the second away leg semi-final versus Dinamo Bucharest. In the final in Rome, he was successful from the penalty spot as the Reds won the shoot-out 4-2 to be crowned Champions of Europe. 47 goals, Footballer of the Year and PFA Player of the Year as Joe Fagan's side won a trophy treble.

Defending the trophy, he scored a six-yard box hat-trick versus Benfica at a rain soaked Anfield and found the net twice in the semi-final versus Panathinaikos. In the final versus Juventus, there was the tragedy of Heysel.

With Liverpool FC and English clubs now banned from Europe, Rush's strike partner was also now his player/manager, Kenny Dalglish. In the 1985/86 season, Rush scored 33 goals as the double was won. He scored 22 in the league. In the FA Cup he scored both semi-final goals versus Peter Shilton in a 2-0 victory versus Southampton at White Hart Lane. In the first all-Merseyside FA Cup Final, he scored another brace, assisted by Jan Molby and Ronnie Whelan as the Reds beat Everton 3-1 to the complete the league and cup double.

In the summer Juventus bid a British record £3.2 million for Rush.

With Juve having their quota of two foreign players, he was loaned back to Liverpool for the 1986/87 season. Far from easing up, Rushie scored 40 goals! 30 in the league, including a hat-trick versus Leicester City. He became the first player to record 30 top-flight league goals in two separate seasons since Jimmy Greaves in the early/mid 1960s.

In the League Cup Final, he scored to put the Reds one up versus Arsenal, who came back to win; for the first time in 146 games Liverpool had lost a match in which Rush had scored. He scored twice in his final Merseyside derby at Anfield and in his final home game scored the only goal of the game versus Watford.

In the 1987/88 season with Juventus, he scored 14 goals, including 8 in 29 Serie A appearances. Although he had scored as many goals as Marco Van Basten, with Liverpool having first refusal, he returned to Anfield in August 1988 for a club record £2.7m.

In the 1988/89 season, returning from an injury lay off, as substitute Number 14 he came off the bench to score twice versus Everton to win the FA Cup Final – 3-2 after extra time.

In the 1990 FA Cup semi-final he put the Reds one up versus Crystal Palace but had to leave the field injured. In his absence Liverpool lost 4-3. In the league he scored 18 goals including vital comeback strikes versus Southampton and QPR at Anfield as Liverpool won the title in 1989/90 for an eighteen time, claiming a fifth championship winner's medal.

Following the resignation of Dalglish and the appointment of Graeme Souness, Rush scored his fifth FA Cup Final goal as the Reds beat Sunderland 2-0 in the 1992 Cup Final. At the start of the 1993/94 season he was appointed captain.

In the final Merseyside derby in front of a standing Kop in March 1994 the teams were led out by entertainer and fund-raiser Roy Castle with captains Rush and Watson both scoring. In season 1994/95, under Roy Evans, he scored a hat-trick away to Blackburn in the League Cup. The final at Wembley saw the Reds beat Bolton 2-1 with skipper Rush delighted: "The sense of pride at actually lifting the trophy was immense and it's something I will never forget."

Rush's second farewell season with the Reds in 1995/96 saw him break Denis Law's FA Cup goalscoring record with one of seven versus Rochdale in a Third Round tie at Anfield. His final game at Anfield was versus Middlesbrough where he was given a guard of honour. In his last game for Liverpool the Reds lost the FA Cup Final to Manchester United.

Rush joined Leeds United, scoring 3 league goals in 36 appearances, often playing wide on the right of midfield. He moved to Newcastle United where he scored in the League Cup to equal Geoff Hurst's competition record and in January 1998, with Kenny Dalglish as manager, combining with John Barnes, he scored his final goal in English football in a Third Round FA Cup tie versus Everton at Goodison Park.

He had further spells with Sheffield United, Wrexham and Sydney Olympic, where he scored his 383rd and final goal in club football.

He hit another 28 for Wales in 73 internationals. Rush in the red of Wales scored winning goals versus France, away to Italy (while still a Juventus player) and a home double versus Spain. Most famously, in June 1991 he scored the only goal of the game versus World Champions Germany in a European Championship qualifier at Cardiff Arms Park.

He has also been Wales Under-17 manager and coached with Liverpool FC before managing Chester in the 2004/05 season.

In April 2005, before the Liverpool versus Juventus Champions League quarter final first leg at Anfield, Rush, along with former Reds team mate Phil Neal and Juventus' Michel Platini commemorated the first meeting between the clubs since Heysel by remembering with a memorial all the supporters who lost their lives in Brussels on 29th May 1985.

In 2005/06, to celebrate the 125th FA Cup season, Rushie was voted the all-time FA Cup hero through a FA.com poll.

In his time with Liverpool the moustached Rushie has also been nicknamed Tosh and Omar and he now enjoys an ambassadorial role with the club.

All those years ago, when faced with the prospect of life without their Number 9 with a move to Juventus, Liverpool supporters organised a 'Rush Must Stay' campaign. All Liverpudlians knew that their goalscorer was the first line of their defence, closing down defenders, and that their goalscorer quite incredibly almost guaranteed happy Saturday afternoons and glorious European football nights. "Ian Rush, Ian Rush, Ian, Ian Rush, he gets the ball, he scores a goal, Ian, Ian Rush."

Premier League Era

The Premiership kicked off in August 1992. The Football League consisting of Division One, (which in time became the Championship), Division Two (League 1) and Division Three (League 2).

Where once perhaps we had to wait for confirmation of a goalscorer until we picked up our copy of our local evening football paper, now stadium announcers and names on backs of shirts from 1993/94 made the identity of all goalscorers immediate and without doubt.

The Jean-Marc 'Bosman' ruling gave freedom of transfer and increased player power.

Football Coming Home was celebrated at Euro '96.

As football entered the 21st century, more and more recognition was given to goals scored in the top flight, as players' individual scoring records were defined by goals scored in the Premier League, post-Football League. Some things though never change, as approaching his 40th year and in a third decade of goalscoring over 19 seasons, John Aldridge, now at Tranmere Rovers was still finding the net.

The Premier League is now in its 30th season and the British game is now the most popular sporting attraction in the world, with global television audiences exceeding the millions of supporters who go to the match, with England's main domestic competition at the very centre of attention.

Goalscorers of the time included:

'Super' Kevin Phillips: European Golden Shoe winner 1999/2000 for Sunderland with 30 league goals, to date the only English winner of this award.

Shaun Goater, cult hero at Rotherham United, Bristol City, Manchester City ('Feed the goat and he will score') and Southend United.

Jermaine Defoe with over 300 career goals for seven clubs, including Spurs, Toronto FC and Rangers.

Jordan Rhodes: goals kingpin with 200 plus career goals before the age of 30.

Dean Saunders: over 200 club goals and 22 international goals for Wales.

Phil Stant 'ooh ah Stantona!', a Falklands veteran and scorer of over 200 goals in league and non-league football.

Guy Whittingham, the only goalscorer during this era to score 40 league goals in a single season in England, achieving so at Portsmouth with 42 in 1992/93. In 1993/94, David Taylor scored 43 league goals for Porthmadog in the Cymru Premier to be Europe's leading goalscorer. From 1996/97, a weighted points system was introduced based on UEFA ranking with a goal = to 2 points in the major European leagues.

Glenn Ferguson 'Spike' scored over 500 Irish League and cup goals.

David Healy, although not a prolific scorer at club level, sits equal 7th with Gareth Bale on the all-time list of British international goalscorers with 36 goals, including a European Championship group qualifying record 13 for Northern Ireland ahead of Davor Suker and Robert Lewandowski.

Billy Sharp, who has scored more English league goals than anyone in the 21st century with 235 league goals (and counting) with eight clubs including over 100 for Sheffield United.

Rickie Lambert was the previous record holder with 219 English league goals with nine clubs, including over 100 for Southampton.

Teddy Sheringham, deep-lying centre forward, over 250 league goals, mostly for Millwall, Spurs and Manchester United, first Premier League Golden Boot winner.

Scottish international Kenny Miller scored over 200 goals for a dozen club sides.

Glenn Murray, again with over 200 goals across the leagues, including for Brighton and Crystal Palace.

Darren Bent scored over 200 career goals for nine clubs, including 106 Premier League goals for six different clubs.

With thirteen league clubs, Jamie Cureton has scored over 250 goals.

Charlie Austin, with over 200 career goals and still scoring in a second spell with QPR.

Dutch Superstars: Ruud van Nistelrooy, in just five seasons with Manchester United, scored 150 goals in only 219 appearances. Jimmy Floyd Hasselbaink a fans' favourite with Leeds United, Chelsea and Middlesbrough, and Robin van Persie, Golden Boot winner in consecutive seasons with Arsenal and Manchester United.

Didier Drogba: the first African footballer to score 100 league goals in England and a record breaking 9 Cup Final goals for Chelsea in the

League Cup, FA Cup and Champion League Finals.

In separate spells with Liverpool, clinical finishers Fernando Torres 'El Niño' the kid and Luis Suarez, European Golden Shoe winner with both the Reds and Barcelona.

Romelu Lukaku, returning to English football, having already scored 146 goals previously, and also over 100 combined in Belgium and Italy.

Captain Troy Deeney, 140 goals for Watford FC, now playing for Birmingham City.

Danny Ings of Aston Villa, following a summer move from Southampton.

A trio of Golden Boot winners: Pierre-Emerick Aubameyang, Sadio Mane and Mo Salah, who took only 162 games to reach 100 Premier league goals.

Sergio Aguero

"He is a legend, and part of history in the club. Aguero's numbers speak for themselves – he is amazing." – Pep Guardiola

"Just a wonderful all-round centre forward who has been brilliant for Manchester City and the Premier League." – Alan Shearer.

Sergio 'Kun' Aguero, 184: most Premier League goals for a single club as the top scoring overseas player and Manchester City record league goalscorer.

12 – most hat-tricks in the Premier League. 260 – most goals for a single club in the Premier League era and Manchester City record goalscorer in all competitions. Premier League Golden Boot winner. Five consecutive seasons with 20 or more Premier League goals, 2014/15 to 2018/19 (only Thierry Henry can match this record).

43 – club record European goals for City. Five Premier league titles – 2011/12, 2013/14, 2017/18, 2018/19, 2020/21. FA Cup – 2019. League Cup 2014, 2016, 2018, 2019, 2020.

Manchester City's number 10 out of 10 – Sergio Leonel Aguero Del Castillo.

The 'Kun' is a nickname from his resemblance to a Japanese cartoon character called Kum-Kum from his favourite series as a child. "My grandparents were the first ones who gave me the name... and so I have grown to appreciate it because it's unique."

In 1998, Aguero entered the youth system of Independiente de Avellaneda. "Football surrounds you in Argentina and so I began playing at a very young age, as soon as class ended in Quilmes in Buenos Aires, my friends and I would start up a game."

In July 2003, just a month after his fifteenth birthday, he became the youngest debutant in the Argentinian First Division as a substitute for Independiente against San Lorenzo, breaking the record of Diego Armando Maradona. Two years later, in 2005, he won the Under-20 World Cup with Argentina.

After 23 goals in 56 appearances for Independiente he moved to Atletico Madrid in June 2006 for 23 million euros. With the 'Rojiblancos' he scored 101 goals, with 74 in 175 La Liga appearances, including twice hitting doubles versus Barcelona. In 2010 the Europa League was won, beating Fulham in the final in Hamburg. In season 2010/11 he scored 20 La Liga goals, 27 in total including in the UEFA Super Cup Final in Monaco in a 2-0 victory versus Inter Milan.

In July 2011 he joined Manchester City, signing for Roberto Mancini's

'Citizens' for £35 million. He made his Premier League debut in August, scoring twice as a substitute in a 4-0 win versus Swansea City, tweeting afterwards: "Very happy with my debut for City, hopefully the start of something big. Thank you to my team mates and the fans for their support."

In September he scored his first Premier League hat-trick in 3-0 victory versus Wigan Athletic and the following month, in his first Manchester derby, he scored in a 6-1 away win, United's worst home debut at Old Trafford since February 1955 (when City had won 5-0).

Going into the 38th and final Premier League game of the season on Sunday 13th May 2012, City and United were level on 86 points. United won at Sunderland, whilst City, playing QPR at the Etihad Stadium, scored a late equaliser through Dzeko, then on 93:20 Martin Tyler's commentary, "Agueroooooooooo!" Sergio scored his 30th goal of the season to win City their first Premier League title and first top-flight league title for 44 years, since the 1967/68 side.

"In my career so far it's the most important goal, you score the goal in the last minute to win the title, I wish I could you tell you how I did it, but I can't... it fell at my feet and I just thought, 'hit the target, hit it as hard as you can, hit the target and it went in'."

In season 2013/14, under Manuel Pellegrini, Aguero scored 28 goals, including 17 in 23 Premier League appearances as the Premier League was regained after finishing as runners-up the previous season to United. In the league he scored twice in the Manchester derby 4-1 win and the League Cup was won against Sunderland 3-1 after Aguero, returning from injury, had scored versus West Ham in the semi-final.

In 2014/15 he was the Premier League Golden Boot winner with 26 Premier League goals in 33 appearances. He hit four versus Spurs in October and in May a hat-trick versus QPR. In total he scored 32 goals in all competitions with a Champions League hat-trick versus Bayern Munich in the group stages.

In 2015/16 he scored 24 Premier League goals in 30 appearances, becoming only the fifth player in Premier League history to score five in game, in the 6-1 win versus Newcastle United in October. He also scored all three in the victory over Chelsea in April. The League Cup was won with Aguero scoring in the semi-final versus Everton and he was successful from the penalty spot in the shoot-out win over Liverpool (3-1) in the final.

He scored a personal best 33 goals in Pep Guardiola's first season in charge in 2016/17, which included two hat-tricks in the Champions League versus Steaua Bucharest and Borussia Monchengladbach.

In October 2017 Aguero suffered injured ribs in a car crash in an Amsterdam taxi, but the following month he overtook Eric Brook's club goalscoring record with his 178th City goal in the Champions League versus Napoli; in time he would also overtake Brook's and Tommy Johnson's 158 league goals. In season 2017/18 he scored 30 goals, with 21 in 25 Premier League appearances. The League Cup was retained, with Aguero scoring in both semi-final legs versus Bristol City and again in the final versus Arsenal (3-0). He scored hat-tricks in the league in the 6-0 away win at Watford and the 3-1 home win versus Newcastle, City winning the Premier League with a record 100 points and record 106 goals.

The following season a historic treble was achieved. In the League Cup he scored in the penalty shoot-out victory over Chelsea (4-3) and was an unused sub in the FA Cup Final triumph over Watford. The quadruple was denied, as Aguero scored in the Champions League quarter-final defeat to Spurs. The Premier League was secured with another last day title victory, this time away to Brighton, with Sergio scoring in a 4-1 win to give City the crown by one point from Liverpool. During the season he had scored three Premier League hat-tricks, versus Huddersfield Town (6-1) and in one week in February 2019 versus Arsenal (3-1) and Chelsea (6-0).

In January 2020 he scored his 12th Premier League hat-trick versus Aston Villa in a 6-1 away win, to overtake Alan Shearer's record of eleven. In March he again scored versus Villa in the League Cup Final victory.

With his Manchester City contract not being renewed beyond the 2020/21 season, his final season with City was restricted by injuries, contracting coronavirus and City playing a system without a recognised striker. He played his final Premier League match for City in a 5-0 win versus Everton at the Etihad Stadium. There was a pre-match guard of honour before, as a second half substitute, he scored twice to take his Premier League tally with City to 184 goals in 275 appearances.

One week later Aguero made his final appearance in a City shirt as a late substitute in the Champions League Final defeat to Chelsea in Porto. His City all competitions records reads: 260 goals in 390 appearances. In his club career he has totalled 384 goals, with more to come as a

Barcelona player from the 2021/22 season.

With Argentina he won a second Under-20 World Cup in 2007 and an Olympic Gold Medal at Beijing 2008. For the senior side he has scored 42 goals, only behind Messi and Batistuta from 101 international appearances. He has played at three World Cups: South Africa 2010 under coach Maradona, Brazil 2014 where he scored in the penalty shoot-out semi-final win over Holland before losing to Germany in the World Cup Final and in Russia 2018 where he scored twice.

On the Manchester City home shirt for season 2021/22, '93:20' shall be featured in honour and appreciation of the club's greatest moment from their greatest goalscorer – with a promise of a statue on the way.

In his Instagram post, Sergio shared: "A huge sense of satisfaction and pride remains in me for having played with Manchester City for a whole 10 seasons... with major achievements, throughout which I became top goalscorer, forging an indestructible bond with all those who love this club – people who will always be in my heart."

As the banner at his final home game at the Etihad read: 'Thank you Sergio, you changed our lives.'

Steve Bull

In the history of English football, Steve Bull is the one player with 50 goals in successive seasons. In 1987/88 and 1988/89, 30 years on from Wolves winning successive top-flight league titles, 100 years on from the formation of the Football League, he struck 52 and 50 league and cup goals in the black and gold of Wolverhampton Wanderers.

In 1987/88 he was the first player since Terry Bly for Peterborough in 1960/61 to score 50 plus goals in a season. In 1988/89 he became the first since George Camsell for Middlesbrough in 1926/27 and 1927/28 to score a century of goals in consecutive seasons.

With Wolves, Bully holds the club records for most goals in all competitions with 306, most league goals 250, most goals in a season 52 and most hat-tricks 18. The only one he does not have is most league goals in a season. Dennis Westcott with 38 as the First Division top scorer in 1946/47 season holds that club record, Bully's personal best is 37!

From Tipton, Staffordshire, Steve played for local junior teams Red Lion and Newey Goodman. After leaving school he joined West Midlands outfit Tipton Town where his various part-time jobs to make ends meet included "mucking the pigs out at my mate's farm to get me fit in pre-season".

Tipton manager Sid Day was also a scout for West Bromwich Albion and Bully was signed by the Baggies in August 1985. "I was doing 13 hours a day in a factory and then training Tuesday and Thursday night with the youth team at Albion, I left my job to go and play football."

Over a season and a half in the First and Second Division with West Brom he had three managers, Johnny Giles, Nobby Stiles and Ron Saunders, scoring 3 goals in 9 appearances, 2 goals in 4 league appearances. Released by Saunders, he was signed by Wolves in November 1986 along with Andy Thompson for £65,000. Manager Graham Turner shared his vision for the club with Steve. "When I see Graham, I shake his hand about that."

Bull was joining Wolves in their first season in club history in the fourth tier of English football. Almost immediately 'The Tipton Skin' (a nickname picked up for his accent and crew cut hairstyle) set about putting things right.

He scored his first Wolves goal in December 1986 in the Freight Rover Trophy away to Cardiff City. His first Wolves league goal was eleven days later in a 1-0 away win at Hartlepool, whom he would also score his first Wolves hat-trick against in a 4-1 win at Molineux on the final day of the league season.

Finishing fourth in the table in the first season of the play-offs, 1986/87, Bull scored in the semi-final away leg to Colchester but Wolves lost the play-off final 3-0 on aggregate to Aldershot.

In season 1987/88 he was the Football League top scorer with 34 league goals, including hat-tricks versus Exeter 4-2 away and in a 5-3 home win versus Darlington as Wolves won the Fourth Division championship. He also scored 3 goals in both the FA Cup and League Cup and 12 in the Sherpa Van Trophy, including 3 goals in both legs of the semi-final versus Notts County.

In the final at Wembley, before a crowd of 80,000, Wolves beat Burnley 2-0 with Bully's strike partner Andy Mutch among the goals.

In the 1988/89 season, Bully was again the Football League top scorer with 37 league goals, including a four-goal haul versus Preston North End in a 6-0 win as Wolves won the Third Division championship. He also scored twice in the League Cup and eleven goals in the Sherpa Van Trophy to bring up the 50!

With 102 goals over two seasons, and Under-21 and England B recognition, Bull joined a select band of Third Division footballers to be awarded a full England cap. He made his international debut versus Scotland in the Rous Cup at Hampden Park in May 1989, as a substitute for John Fashanu, partnering Tony Cottee up front. Bully marked the occasion by scoring, controlling and drilling the ball past Jim Leighton, in doing so emulating the great Tommy Lawton as an international goalscorer for England whilst playing for a Third Division side. In April 1990 Steve scored twice at Wembley versus Czechoslovakia in a 4-2 win. In June, in a World Cup warm up match in Tunis, he scored in a 1-1 draw versus Tunisia.

At Italia '90, Bull featured briefly in all three England group games, with Jimmy Greaves revealing a T-shirt in the television studio: 'Let the Bull Loose'. He went on to play in the last 16 victory over Belgium. In total, under Bobby Robson and Graham Taylor, he won 13 international caps, scoring 4 goals.

In October 1989, Bull scored a late winner in the first Black Country derby match for five years as Wolves returned to the Second Division with a 2-1 win at the Hawthorns. On New Year's Day 1990 'Ooh Bully Bully' was the cry as he hit Newcastle for four away at St. James Park, finishing the season with 24 league goals.

In 1990/91 he hit 26 league goals, including a hat-trick in a 4-0 victory against Bristol City. In four seasons Bully had scored 121 league goals!

In 1992, he scored his 195th Wolves goal to overtake previous club record holder John Richards.

In seasons 1994/95 and 1996/97, under managers Graham Taylor and Mark McGhee, Wolves reached the play-offs. In 1995, after finishing 4th in the league, Bull scored in the semi-final home leg versus Bolton as Wolves lost 3-2 on aggregate. In 1997, with a league position of 3rd Wolves lost in the semi-finals 4-3 on aggregate to Crystal Palace. That same year, he was awarded a testimonial with Wolves playing Santos of Brazil at Molineux.

Bull's final two seasons with Wolves, under Colin Lee, were hampered by knee injuries. In season 1998/99 he scored his final Wolves goals. His final hat-trick was in August 1998 in a League cup tie versus Barnet in a 5-0 win at Molineux. His final goal in black and gold was in the 1-0 home win versus Bury in the league in September 1998.

In 1999, at the age of 34 Steve retired from Wolverhampton Wanderers and league football. In 2001 he made several appearances and scored for Hereford United in the Conference League. He also had a spell as manager of Stafford Rangers in the Blue Square North League.

In 2003 the John Ireland Stand at Molineux was renamed the Steve Bull Stand and in July 2006 Steve was made honorary vice-president of Wolverhampton Wanderers Football Club.

Presently Wolves are an established Premier League club. 35 years ago, when Steve Bull joined, the club was almost down and out. Bully's goals restored pride and profile, even appearing on *A Question of Sport* and *Football Focus*. 306 Wolves goals in 561 appearances. 250 Wolves league goals in 474 appearances.

With a promise of goals, Bully's loyalty delivered a dream to all Wolves followers. Today his good works continue through The Steve Bull Foundation, supporting charitable causes in the Black Country and the West Midlands.

Andrew Cole

In 1993/94 Andy Cole raised the bar for modern day goalscoring. With an outstanding 34 Premier League goals, the most in the top flight of English football since Ron Davies of Southampton in 1966/67 and still the highest number of goals scored in a Premier League season, equalled only by Alan Shearer.

From a Caribbean background, his father had a passion for cricket, his mother remembers a young Andrew always having a football by his side. He was given great encouragement by his grandad Vincent to make it as a professional footballer.

Growing up in Lenton, South Nottingham, he played for local sides

Padstow United and JCS Garages and met Forest manager Brian Clough, whom his grandad admired.

He was picked up by Arsenal: Chief Scout Terry Murphy visited the Cole family home on his 14th birthday. He signed schoolboy forms and left Nottingham for the FA's National School at Lilleshall.

In 1989 he signed professional terms with the Gunners and over three seasons he twice played for the first team, once in the league and as a late substitute in the shared 1991 Charity Shield v Spurs at Wembley.

During the 1991/92 season he was sent on loan to Third Division Fulham, scoring 3 league goals in 13 appearances and also to Second Division Bristol City. Impressing at Ashton Gate he was signed for a club record £500,000. "For me to come to Bristol City at that time was a massive part of my career, I am forever indebted to them... Personally without this, I don't think I would have achieved what I did in my career."

With 20 league goals in 41 appearances for Denis Smith's side and a hat-trick versus Cardiff City in the League Cup, Newcastle United put in a club record bid of £1.75m and Cole flew the Robins nest to join the Magpies in February 1993. With 12 league goals in 12 appearances, including a hat-trick in the final game of the season in the 7-1 victory over Leicester City, Kevin Keegan's exciting side won promotion as champions.

In his first run of games in top-flight football, he was the Premier League top scorer for season 1993/94 with 34 league goals. In total he scored a club record 41 league and cup goals, surpassing Hughie Gallacher's previous club best. Newcastle finished third in the league, their highest position since Gallacher's goals had fired the Geordies to the 1926/27 league title.

Cole was voted Young Player of the Year. His Premier League goals tally included a first half hat-trick versus Liverpool and goals versus both Arsenal and Manchester United.

In January 1995, after the Third Round of the FA Cup, his Newcastle record read: 55 league goals in 70 appearances, 68 goals in all competitions from 84 games. To everyone's surprise, two days later he was sold to Manchester United for a British record fee of £7m which included Keith Gillespie heading to Tyneside. Manager Keegan, with trusted assistant Terry McDermott, fronted up to supporters on the stadium steps of St. James Park to justify the sale of Newcastle's star striker.

In the foreword of Andrew Cole's autobiography *Fast Forward*, Alex

Ferguson wrote: "I felt we needed someone with an electricity in and around the penalty box, that man was Andy Cole and it changed our attacking dramatically. His overall contribution at United is something I will always be thankful for and in my book he deservedly joins the pantheon of our great players."

Andrew Cole reached such a status by scoring 121 United goals with 93 Premier league goals in 195 appearances. In his time at Old Trafford, he won five Premier League titles – 1995/96, 1996/97, 1998/99, 1999/2000 and 2000/2001, two FA Cups, 1996 and 1999, and a Champions League in 1999.

Just two months after signing, in March 1995 he became the first player in Premier league history to score five goals in a single game, in the 9-0 victory versus Ipswich Town at Old Trafford. In season 1995/96 the double was won, after United had just missed out on both trophies the previous season. The Premier League was won by four points from Newcastle. In the FA Cup, Cole scored in the semi-final victory versus Chelsea and Liverpool were defeated in the final.

In April 1997 he scored a crucial goal at Anfield as United went on to retain the Premier League title. In 1998/99, with new strike partner Dwight Yorke, Cole scored vital goals at home and in Europe.

In the Premier League his winner versus Spurs on the final day of the season secured the title. A week later, United won the FA Cup versus Newcastle for another double. In the Champions League, he scored in the away 3-3 draw with Barcelona, in the semi-finals with United 2-0 down to Juventus in Turin and trailing 3-1 on aggregate, inspired by Roy Keane, their deficit was overturned with Cole scoring a late winner to make it 3-2 to United on the night and 4-3 on aggregate. Returning to the Nou Camp for the final, late goals again versus Bayern Munich in a 2-1 triumph saw United win their first European Cup since Matt Busby's side in 1968. Cole's goals had seen United become the first English side to win the treble of League, FA Cup and European Cup in the same season.

At the start of season 1999/2000 he bagged four in a 5-1 victory over Newcastle. The Premier League was retained and with United competing in the FIFA Club World cup they did not enter the FA Cup. The Intercontinental Cup was also won.

In his final full season with United in 2000/2001, the Premier League was won for a third consecutive season, the first United side in club history to win three top-flight titles in a row. While at Old Trafford, Cole won all his 15 England caps under five managers – Venables, Hoddle, Wilkinson, Keegan and Eriksson. He made his debut in March 1995 as a substitute for Teddy Sheringham versus Uruguay at Wembley. He scored his one international goal in a World Cup qualifier in Tirana versus Albania in March 2001.

With the arrival of Ruud van Nistelrooy, he moved on to Blackburn Rovers under Graeme Souness in December 2001, two months after his 30th birthday, for £8m. In the new year he scored in both semi-final legs of the League Cup versus Sheffield Wednesday in a 6-3 aggregate win. At the Millennium Stadium, Cardiff in February 2002 he scored the winning goal in a 2-1 victory over Spurs and former team-mate Sheringham to give Blackburn their first domestic cup since the 1928 FA Cup.

Joined by his friend Dwight Yorke the following season, Cole scored again in the semi-finals of the League Cup, this time denied over two legs by former club Manchester United.

In two and a half seasons with Rovers he scored 27 league goals in 83 appearances before re-joining Fulham (now in the Premier League) in 2004. Under Chris Coleman he scored a further 12 league goals in 31 appearances.

There were then moves to Manchester City managed by Stuart Pearce, 9 league goals in 22 appearances, Portsmouth (two spells – 3 goals in 18 appearances) either side of playing for Birmingham City, 1 goal in 5 games, Sunderland, 0 from 7 and Burnley, 6 league goals in 13 games including a hat-trick away to QPR.

In 2008 he retired from league football after making 10 appearances for his home town club Nottingham Forest. 289 career club goals. 229 league goals in 509 appearances.

187 Premier league goals in 414 Premier League appearances. Andrew Cole is the third highest goalscorer in Premier League history. With an independent inner self-belief in his football ability, his attitude has often been misunderstood. "I've always been quiet."

He has also worked with Huddersfield Town and Southend and enjoys his role as a club ambassador with Manchester United. He is a pundit on satellite television and with the BBC. With the BAME he helps football communities across the UK and beyond.

In 2015 he suffered renal failure and received a kidney donated by his nephew Alexander. In 2020 he launched, in conjunction with Kidney Research UK, the Andy Cole Fund with the message, "I want to help people".

Robbie Fowler

With the Midas touch to do wonderful things, Robbie Fowler was called 'God'. On his podcast (godcast), he recollects it was his Anfield team mate Neil 'Razor' Ruddock who first gave him the title. Liverpool supporters instantly adopted the nickname, Kopites bestowing complete celestial adoration upon their local hero.

From Toxteth, Liverpool 8, a natural footballing talent was nurtured and honed on the streets and playing fields through practice, practice, and practice.

A childhood Evertonian, his favourites were Graeme Sharp and Trevor Steven, with an admiration for Liverpool's Ian Rush. Playing for junior teams Singleton and Thorvald he was known as Robert Ryder (his mum's name), it was only when he began secondary school and training at Liverpool Football Club's Centre of Excellence after being discovered by youth scout Jim Aspinall, that he started using Fowler (his dad's name) because it sounded more like a footballer – a goalscorer.

In April 1989, just after his fourteen birthday, he was taken on associate schoolboy terms by the Reds and three years later signed his first professional contract.

In September 1993, aged eighteen, Fowler was given his first team debut by manager Graeme Souness, scoring away to Fulham in a League Cup Second Round 1st leg match at Craven Cottage. In October, in his first Premier League match at Anfield, after clattering into Arsenal captain Tony Adams, the Kop chanted "There's only one Robbie Fouler!" Three days later, in the return match versus Fulham, Fowler bagged all five goals in a 5-0 win. "After the Fulham game, I went round the chippy with my mates and got a big kiss from my mum when I got home." In the Reds' next home match, Robbie was the cover star on the Anfield Review Programme and scored his first Premier League goal versus Oldham and completed the month by scoring his first Premier League hat-trick in a 4-2 win versus Southampton at Anfield.

With Roy Evans now in charge, Fowler scored the winner in his first Merseyside derby, the last played before a standing Spion Kop in March 1994. A month later, on Saturday 30th April, he played at Anfield in the 'Kop's Last Stand' match versus Norwich City, the last game in front of the famous terrace.

In August 1994, in Liverpool's first home match before an all-seated Anfield, he scored a hat-trick in a record 4 minutes 33 seconds versus Arsenal. Prior to the match he had been fooling with Ian Wright over Wrighty's tattoos, now Robbie had already left an indelible mark on football history. An ever present in the league, in 42 games he scored 25 goals with a total of 31 goals in all competitions. In the League Cup semi-finals versus Crystal Palace, he scored the only goals of the tie in both legs. At Wembley he won his first winner's medal as the Reds beat Bolton Wanderers 2-1 and Robbie was voted Young Player of the Year.

In the following season, 1995/96, he again was Young Player of the Year. Sporting a peroxide blond dyed hairstyle he hit four versus Bolton in the Premier League in a 5-2 win in September at Anfield. In another ever-present league season, he scored 28 Premier League goals in 38 appearances with 36 goals in total. He found the net in both Premier League games versus Manchester United, scoring twice in the 2-2 draw at Old Trafford (in the high profile return from suspension of Eric Cantona). He also scored twice at Anfield, including a wonderful free kick in a 2-0 win. With his goal celebrations Robbie enjoyed reminding United supporters how many European Cups Liverpool had won. In the FA Cup semi-final, he again struck twice at Old Trafford, this time versus Aston Villa. In the final, versus Man Utd, there would be no goal celebrations, only despondency as Liverpool lost to Cantona's only goal of the game.

At the start of the 1996/97 season, with the legendary Ian Rush having now departed, Fowler swapped his Number 23 shirt for the Number 9 jersey.

In December 1996, he recorded another four-goal league haul, in a 5-1 home win versus Middlesbrough. Into the new year, he had an eventful spring. In March, he scored twice in the European Cup Winners' Cup at Anfield versus Brann Bergen, revealing a T-shirt in support of the striking Liverpool dockers. In the Monday night football game at Highbury versus Arsenal he was seemingly brought down by keeper David Seaman, Fowler pleaded with the referee (Gerald Ashby) it was not a foul. A penalty was still awarded and his spot-kick was saved, with Jason McAteer following up to score from the rebound.

Liverpool Football Club received a fax from FIFA commending Fowler for his sportsmanship. The next day after the fax, he received a letter from UEFA, fining him £1,000 for displaying a political slogan in his support of the dockers! In April, the day after the Hillsborough anniversary, the Reds' challenge for the Premier League all but ended with a 1-1 draw versus Everton at Goodison Park as Fowler twice hit the woodwork and was sent off, thus missing the Reds' remaining league fixtures. A week later he scored in the semi-final of the Cup Winners' Cup second leg in a 2-0 Anfield victory against Paris St. Germain, but it was not enough as the Reds lost out 3-2 on aggregate.

Over the next three seasons, injuries and the immergence of Michael Owen saw Fowler's first team appearances limited, but he still managed Premier League hat-tricks versus Aston Villa (4-2) and Southampton (7-1).

In the 2000/2001 season, under manager Gérard Houllier, Fowler captained the Reds to a historic cup treble. In the League Cup semi-final versus Palace, he scored in the Anfield second leg (5-0) to complete a 6-2 aggregate score line.

In the final at the Millennium Stadium, Cardiff, versus Birmingham City, Fowler scored with a long-range effort, and also in the penalty shoot-out victory and was awarded the Alan Hardaker Trophy for being Man of the Match. In the FA Cup semi-final at Villa Park, he scored a free kick versus Wycombe Wanderers to secure a 2-1 win, with the final won versus Arsenal. In the UEFA Cup Final versus Alaves, at the Westfalenstadion in Dortmund, coming on as a substitute he dribbled through the Spanish defence to give Liverpool a 4-3 lead, eventually the Reds winning 5-4 with a Golden Goal (own goal) in extra time. Three days later, at The Valley, versus Charlton, he scored twice including an overhead kick for Liverpool to finish the season in the Champions League places.

In October 2001 he scored a hat-trick in the Premier League in a 4-1 away win at Leicester City. A month later, despite an outcry on Merseyside, Fowler was sold to Leeds United for a club record £11.75m. With Leeds he scored 14 league goals in 30 games including a Boxing Day hat-trick in his first season versus Bolton.

In 2003, he was bought by Manchester City, netting 21 league goals in 80 appearances, linking up with Kevin Keegan and former team mate and friend Steve McManaman. In December 2003, he scored his one and only goal versus Liverpool in a 2-2 draw at the City of Manchester Stadium. In January 2006 he scored a hat-trick versus Scunthorpe in the FA Cup Third Round and a week later a goal versus United in a 3-1 City win.

Later that same month, Rafael Benitez brought Fowler back. "I honestly don't believe that I have ever been happier in my football life than the moment when I sat in my car outside Anfield, a minute after I had put pen to paper to bring me home." In his second coming, he again opened his account versus Fulham, in a Premier League game at Anfield in February 2006. 'Fowler God 11 Welcome Back to Heaven' read the banner on the Kop. In his second season, exchanging the Number 11 shirt for Number 9 again, player and supporters savoured every moment. Robbie reflected, "I'm just glad I got the opportunity because Liverpool means everything to me." Fowler completed his Liverpool playing career with 128 Premier League goals in 266 appearances, 183 goals in all competitions in 369 games.

He moved to Championship side Cardiff City and, as fate would have it, the Bluebirds were drawn away to Liverpool in the League Cup. On 31st October 2007, Robbie received a rapturous Anfield reception, at the end of the match swapping shirts with Reds' skipper Steven Gerrard.

In 2008/09 he returned to the Premier League with Blackburn Rovers, making three appearances under former Anfield team mate Paul Ince. He also played in Australia for North Queensland Fury and Perth Glory and as player/manager in Thailand with Muangthang United.

He also had coaching spells with MK Dons and Bury and managed Down Under with Brisbane Roar, and with SC East Bengal in the Indian Super League, both times with long-time friend and right-hand man Tony Grant.

In the Premier League, Fowler scored 163 goals in 379 appearances plus a further 4 league goals in 13 Championship games with Cardiff, 231 league and cup goals in total.

At international level, there were 7 England goals in 26 games. He made his England debut versus Bulgaria at Wembley in March 1996. He made two appearances at Euro '96, versus Holland and Spain. His first international goal was in March 1997 at Wembley versus Mexico and he also played in the 2002 World Cup Last 16 match versus Denmark.

In 2014 Robbie had a cameo role in the film *One Night in Istanbul*. In 2006 he had scored twice at the Ataturk Stadium in the Champions League versus Galatasaray. The previous year he was there as a supporter to witness the Reds' historic comeback versus AC Milan, 'The Miracle of Istanbul'.

Fowler has also scored in all three Liverpool Legends matches staged at Anfield, versus Real Madrid, Bayern Munich and AC Milan.

In May 2021, Fowler, with Jamie Carragher, announced the Fowler-Carragher Academy at Liverpool's old training ground at Melwood. "It's a special place, with so much history, and we want to continue that. We are going to be part of a project that is based in the community and offers a real hub for local people."

From the Penny Lane playing fields to Anfield, as much as part of the folklore of Liverpool as The Beatles, Liver Birds and the River Mersey: Growler, the Toxteth Terrier/Terror, breathe right nose strip, whom we saw coming out of HMV in Church Street. In Robbie Fowler, Liverpudlians continue to trust.

Thierry Henry

Once you have seen Thierry Henry play, there is no going back. Except to repeatedly return. The grace, artistry, balance and speed of thought and movement from the French master invites adulation.

"Thierry Henry is probably technically the most gifted footballer ever to play the beautiful game." – Zinedine Zidane

"Sometimes they say God does not give you everything, but Thierry has been given a lot... you couldn't replace him." – Arsène Wenger

A natural dedication has been rewarded with an honours list the length of the Champs-Elysees.

World Cup and European Championship winner. Champions League, Club World Cup, UEFA Super Cup, Ligue 1, Premier League, La Liga, FA Cup, Copa del Rey. European Golden Shoe, Premier League Golden Boot, Footballer of the Year. Ballon d'Or Runner up 2003 and FIFA World Player of the Year Silver Award 2003 and 2004. Surprisingly, the one thing he did not accomplish was to score in a major cup final!

What perhaps supersedes all these achievements is his fight against racism with his Stand Up, Speak Up campaign with black and white interlocking wristbands and his work as a FIFA Fair Play ambassador.

From the multi-cultural Paris suburb of Les Ulis, Henry has always been on his toes. "We didn't even have a remote control! I was the remote, flicking between football and Benny Hill!"

As a junior he registered with CO Les Ulis and also played for Palaiseau and Viry. As a teenager he joined Monaco. In 1994, aged seventeen, he made his debut in Ligue 1 under Arsène Wenger. In 1997 he won the championship and reached the semi-finals of the UEFA Cup. In 1998 he scored versus Juventus in the Champions League semi-finals. Growing up, his idol was AC Milan's Dutch striker Marco van Basten and in January 1999 he followed the same path to Italy, joining Juventus for £10.7m, aged 21. The Italian Job, however, was short lived with 3 goals in 16 Serie A appearances.

In August 1999, Arsène Wenger, now Arsenal manager, brought Henry to North London for £10.5m. Still seeking to find his feet as a goalscorer Wenger moved him from the wing to centre-forward. He scored his first Arsenal goal at Southampton in the league as a substitute in September 1999. It was the start of a beautiful friendship: In his time at Arsenal he scored a club record 228 goals in 377 appearances with 175 Premier League goals in 258 Premier League appearances. In Premier League history is he the sixth highest goalscorer with the best strike rate of 0.68 goals per game.

Henry's Arsenal honours: Premier League, 2001/02, 2003/04. FA Cup, 2002, 2003, 2005. Premier League Golden Boot, 2001/02 (24), 2003/04 (30), 2004/05 (25), 2005/06 (27). Only Jimmy Greaves (six) and Steve Bloomer (five) have been the top-flight leading goalscorer in English football history more times.

European Golden Shoe winner, 2003/04 (30), 2004/05 (25). The only player from the English top flight to be the continental top goalscorer twice. Footballer of the Year, 2002/03, 2003/04 and 2005/06. The only player since the award began in 1947/48 to be a three-time winner.

After defeat in the 2000 UEFA Cup Final on penalties to Galatasaray, when Henry had scored in the semi-finals versus Lens, his first Arsenal winners medals were in the 2001/02 season. when Arsenal won the Premier League and FA Cup double. He scored twice versus title rivals Manchester United in a 3-1 win in the league and Chelsea were beaten in the cup final at the Millennium Stadium.

In 2002/03, the FA Cup was retained versus Southampton and Thierry won the first of successive PFA Player of the Year awards.

In 2003/04, Henry and Arsenal were Premier League 'Invincibles'. The first side in English football history to go through the league season undefeated since Preston North End in the inaugural 1888/89 season, playing 22 league games. Arsenal's record read: Played 38, Won 26, Drew 12. Points 90. Goals for 73, with Thierry astonishingly contributing 30 goals of the league total. In April 2004 he scored seven Premier League goals in a week, a Good Friday hat-trick versus Liverpool (4-2) and four against Leeds United (5-0).

"Coming up against Thierry Henry and 'The Invincibles', I would say that was the most difficult job in football, when he hit top gear and ran past you, it was like trying to chase after someone on a motorbike." – Jamie Carragher.

In Europe he scored twice away to Inter Milan in the Champions League including a solo special in a 5-1 victory, the Arsenal fans singing 'five-one in the San Siro' to the tune of 'one-nil to the Arsenal'. Henry became the first player since Ian Rush in 1983/84 to be Footballer of the Year, PFA Player of the Year, English top-flight leading goalscorer and European Golden Shoe winner, all in the same season.

In October 2005, now Arsenal captain, Henry equalled and broke Ian

Wright's, Arsenal club goalscoring record of 185 with a brace in a Champions League group stage game versus Sparta Prague.

Thierry reflected: "At the beginning, I felt I was more likely to break the clock at Highbury than the record of Wrighty!" It was also to be the start of a Champions League journey all the way to the final in Paris. In the Last 16 he scored one of the most memorable goals in European football with a wonderful solo effort versus Real Madrid in the Bernabeu. In the quarter-finals he laid the ghost of Turin to rest with a goal versus Juventus. In the semi-finals versus Villarreal, a sight even quicker than Thierry Henry was seen at Highbury as a grey squirrel raced across the pitch.

Prior to the final, Arsenal played their last ever game at Highbury on 7th May 2006 before moving to their new stadium. Thierry Henry give the famous old stadium of 93 years the perfect send off. Wearing the red currant strip the Gunners adopted for the season, replicating the Arsenal side from 1913, he delivered a hat-trick versus Wigan Athletic (4-2), including scoring the last goal at Highbury, a penalty in front of the North Bank.

Ten days later, in his home city, there was disappointment again in a European final with a 2-1 defeat to Barcelona.

In an injury plagued final season with Arsenal he scored his 'final goal' for the club in a league draw versus Middlesbrough in February 2007. In the summer, Henry joined the Catalan giants for £16.1m. In three seasons at the Nou Camp he scored 49 goals in 121 games, winning two La Ligas, a Copa del Rey, the Champions League, UEFA Super Cup and FIFA Club World Cup. In the 2008/09 treble season he scored 26 goals in 42 appearances, including twice in the 6-2 away win against Real Madrid and a hat-trick versus Valencia. In the 2009/10 Champions League quarter-final he played for Barcelona against Arsenal at the Emirates.

By the end of the season, in the summer of 2010, Henry departed European football, joining New York Red Bulls in the MLS on Bastille Day.

In January 2012 he returned to Arsenal (on a two-month loan) during the MLS off-season. A month earlier in December 2011, Arsenal unveiled a bronze statue of Henry outside the Emirates Stadium as part of the club's 125 years anniversary celebrations. An Arsenal immortal, he scored his 'final goal' for the club in a 2-1 win over Sunderland in February 2012.

For France, a legendary goalscorer, as his nation's top scorer with 51 international goals from 123 appearances for Les Bleus. A World Cup winner in 1998 (although he did not play in the final). A Euro 2000 winner, including a goal in the semi-final victory over Portugal. At the 2006 World Cup he scored the only goal of the game in the quarter-final versus Brazil and was named in the all-star team of the tournament. The Hand of Gaul incident in the World Cup play-off versus Ireland in 2009 sparked controversy. At international level he has also assisted Belgium. He has also managed his first club Monaco and Montreal Impact in the Canadian League.

With 50 European Cup/Champions League goals he is 7th on the all-time list of top scorers since the competition began in 1955. In European club football he has scored 233 top-flight league goals across the leagues in France, Italy, England and Spain.

In April 2021, the Premier League announced the first inductees of their Hall of Fame and Arsenal's Thierry Henry was top of the list. "To be inducted... into the Premier League Hall of Fame is more than special. When I was young, I was just trying to make sure I could get a pair of boots and now we're talking about the Hall of Fame. During my career I wanted to play hard and make sure I was fighting for the cause, because that's all the fans want to see. It's an amazing honour. One thing is for sure, I wanted to change the game, there's one thing to lift trophies, there's one thing to lead goals, but did you elevate the position that you were playing in?"

Harry Kane

"Buzzing... buzzing to get the first start and to get a goal at White Hart Lane, and to win 5-1 was a brilliant night. As soon as I scored it, the emotions came out, I've been waiting patiently and to get that goal was a proud moment. It's the best feeling of my career without a doubt, hopefully I can push on and get a few more."

Dateline: April 2014 and Harry Kane has just scored his first Premier League top-flight goal for Tottenham Hotspur. An overnight success from when, in January 2011, on loan at League One Leyton Orient he made his Football League debut.

He certainly has pushed on, as a 28-year-old he has a career tally of 280 goals with a strike rate of two goals every three games. England's Number 9 and Spurs' Number 10 is the leading goalscorer of his generation.

How many goals shall Harry Kane have by the time he hangs up his boots? As always, the same variables of form and fitness apply. Almost without exception all the greats of goalscoring including Dean, Greaves, Law, Rush and Shearer have seen their goals return diminish through age and injuries. How many goals shall Harry Kane score? Time will tell.

He has reached his current level through complete dedication, practice and determination. Born in Walthamstow, East London, growing up in Chingford, Essex, he returned to local football, playing for Gladstone Rovers on Saturdays and Ridgeway Rovers on Sundays, after being released by Arsenal, aged nine. Two years later, encouraged by scout Mark O'Toole, Spurs took Kane on, coming through the academy and eventually signing professional terms in 2009.

Unable to make the first team, he joined third tier Leyton Orient on loan. Manager Russell Slade give Kane his senior debut as a substitute for Scott McGleish in a 1-1 draw with Rochdale. A week later he scored his first goal in league football in the 4-0 defeat of Sheffield Wednesday. After five league goals in 18 appearances for the O's he returned to Spurs for the start of the 2011/12 season.

After previous appearances on the bench, he was given his Spurs debut by Harry Redknapp in the Europa League qualifying play-offs versus Hearts at White Hart Lane in August 2011. In December, in the group stages, he scored his first Spurs goal in the final minute of the match in Dublin versus Michael O'Neill's Shamrock Rovers. The following month, in January 2012, he joined Championship side Millwall on loan, scoring 7 league goals in 22 appearances, helping Kenny Jackett's team avoid relegation.

Back at Spurs he made his Premier League debut on the opening day of the 2012/13 season as a late substitute away to Newcastle. By the end of August, he was on loan with fellow Premier League side Norwich City, before an injury saw him return to Spurs to recover. He played three Premier League games for the Canaries without scoring. In February 2013 he was on loan again to Leicester of the Championship, scoring two league goals in 13 appearances. His last game for the Foxes was as a second half substitute in the semi-final play-off defeat to Watford.

2013/14: Under André Villas-Boas, in October, Kane scored his first goal at White Hart Lane in the 2-2 draw with Hull City in the League Cup, he also scored in the 8-7 penalty shoot-out win. The following April 2014, with his one-time Spurs Under-23 coach Tim Sherwood now in charge, he made his first Premier League start, scoring his first Premier League goal in the 5-1 win versus Sunderland. He then found the net again, in his next two matches versus WBA and Fulham, ending the season with 3 Premier league goals from 10 appearances.

At the start of the 2014/15 season, with Mauricio Pochettino now manager, Kane scored a glut of goals in the Europa League and League Cup, including his first hat-trick versus Asteras Tripolis where, after a late red to keeper Hugo Lloris, he went in goal. Although he did not make a Premier League start until November, he still managed 21 Premier League goals with 31 goals in all competitions. Premier League highlights included a double versus Chelsea (5-3) on New Year's Day 2015, both goals versus Arsenal in the North London derby (2-1) and his first Premier League hat-trick (4-3) versus Leicester in March, barely two years on from being on the bench for the Foxes in the Championship play-off semi-final at Vicarage Road. Spurs also reached the League Cup Final, losing to Chelsea 2-0 and Harry was voted PFA Young Player of the Year.

In 2015/16, Kane won his first Premier League Golden Boot as a league ever-present with 25 Premier League goals, including strikes versus Manchester City in a 4-1 home win and a hat-trick away to Bournemouth (5-1) as Spurs challenged for the title all the way to May. A second Golden Boot followed in 2016/17 with 29 Premier League goals from 30 appearances. He hit four Premier League hat-tricks: WBA and Stoke City, both four goals to nil. In the last two games of the season, he scored seven goals in May 2017, both away from home versus Leicester (6-1) where he struck four times and a hat-trick at Hull City (7-1).

He also scored a hat-trick in the FA Cup away to Fulham in the 5th Round. In the quarter-finals he faced old club Millwall, but left the pitch injured early on. "It was a big part of my development, I had a great time at Millwall, I enjoyed my loan spell there, I was eighteen at the time, playing in the Championship, we were in a relegation battle and it really turned me into a man." Kane returned for the cup semi-final at Wembley, scoring in a 4-2 defeat to Chelsea. In the Premier League, Spurs were runners-up, their highest league finish since the 1962/63 season with the goalscoring partnership of Jimmy Greaves and Bobby Smith. In 38 games in all competitions, he scored 35 goals, with goal number 35 coming in the last ever match at White Hart Lane in a 2-1 home victory over Manchester United on 14th May 2017.

In 2017/18 he scored a personal best 41 goals, including 30 in the Premier League. He hit two Premier League hat-tricks in the space of three days in December 2017, away to Burnley (3-0) and at Spurs' temporary Wembley 'home' on Boxing Day, 5-2 versus Southampton. He also scored a Champions League hat-trick away to APOEL in a 3-0 victory in Greece.

In the calendar year of 2017, he recorded a Premier League record of 39 goals in 36 matches, beating Alan Shearer's record of 36 for Blackburn in 1995. Shearer sent Kane congratulations via Twitter. Harry said, "To be compared with Alan Shearer is great." Pep Guardiola called Spurs 'The Harry Kane Team'. His grand total for the year was 56 goals for club and country, including 17 goals in 13 games in September and October. Kane was the first player in a decade (since David Villa) to outscore both Messi and Ronaldo.

In the 2018/19 season, after recovering from injury, he played in Spurs' first European Cup/Champions League final, suffering defeat to Liverpool in Madrid 2-0. In the Premier League season he scored 17 goals in 28 appearances.

In August 2019 he scored his first goals, a brace versus Aston Villa in Spurs' new Tottenham Hotspur Stadium in a 3-1 home victory, with 18 Premier League goals from 29 appearances. Kane landed his third Golden Boot in season 2020/21 with 23 Premier League goals and lost in his third cup final versus Manchester City in the League Cup Final. In the Premier League he scored twice away at Old Trafford in a 6-1 win versus Manchester United in October and in December scored once versus Arsenal in a 2-0 win to become, with 11 eleven goals, the leading goalscorer in North London derbies.

With 14 assists (combining with Son Heung-min) he became the first player since Andy Cole in 1993/94 to top both the Premier League goals and assists charts in the same season. "Harry Kane is a special player in the history of the club, he is one of the best strikers in the world. The team depends a lot on him, we can't hide that. It's the goals he can score, the assists he can make, the link play he has..." – Manager José Mourinho.

Spurs fans sing: "Harry Kane, he's one of our own." 223 goals in 342 appearances, 166 Premier League goals in 246 appearances. With his goalscoring exploits and leadership at international level he is a figurehead for the England national team. He made his debut under Roy Hodgson in a European Championship qualifier versus Lithuania in March 2015, scoring after 79 seconds as a second half substitute for Wayne Rooney. At Euro 2016 he played all four games.

In June 2017 he was appointed skipper by Gareth Southgate. In his first match as captain, he scored in a World Cup qualifier at Hampden Park in a 2-2 draw with Scotland. At World Cup 2018 in Russia, Kane won the Golden Boot with six goals as England reached the semi-finals, defeated by Croatia 2-1 after extra time. He hit a double versus Tunisia (2-1), a hat-trick (the first by an England player at a World Cup Finals since Gary Lineker in Mexico '86) versus Panama (6-1) and goal number six versus Colombia in the Round of 16, where he also scored in the penalty shoot-out (4-3).

In 2019 he scored two Wembley hat-tricks in Euro 2020 qualifiers versus Bulgaria (4-0) and Montenegro (7-0). At the Euros in 2021 Kane scored four times to equal Lineker's England tournament record of ten goals. In the Round of 16 versus Germany (2-1), in the quarter-final in Rome he scored twice versus the Ukraine (4-0) and in the Wembley semi-final he scored the extra-time winner versus Denmark (2-1) to send England to their first final since 1966. He scored in the penalty shoot-out 3-2 loss to Italy after the final had ended 1-1 after extra-time.

A credit to the nation on the football field, he has captained his country 41 times in 64 international appearances. Kane has not forgotten where he has come from, sponsoring the shirts of his old team Leyton Orient. He is also an ambassador for the Tommy Club, a charity which raises funds for ex-servicemen and women.

Harry Kane: Last of the great goalscorers? Targets: trophies and goalscoring records – Spurs goals 223, record – 266 Jimmy Greaves (268 including Charity Shield). Premier League goals 166, record – 260 Alan Shearer. Three times top-flight leading scorer, record – 6 Jimmy Greaves. England goals 41, record – 53 Wayne Rooney.

Silverware and goals: "Good times, never seemed so good."

Henrik Larsson

More than anything, the epic goalscoring of Henrik Larsson restored a paradise lost to Celtic Football Club. His arrival at Parkhead in July 1997 for a bargain £650,000 and subsequent contribution to the cause signalled the end of a decade of Rangers domination, and catapulted Celtic to a first European final in 33 years.

Have boots will travel, he found himself in Glasgow from Sweden via Holland. It was in his blood, his father (surname Rocha) was a sailor from the West African coast Cape Verde Islands. He took his mum's name, Larsson, as a more Swedish name to help repel racial taunting.

In Sweden he played part-time whilst working for a company loading vegetables onto trucks. First for local side Högaborgs, scoring 23 goals in 74 appearances, then, aged 20 in 1991, he joined Second Division Helsingborg. He scored 50 goals in 56 appearances, as his home town team gained promotion to the top flight 'Allsvenskan' for the first time in over 20 years.

In 1993 he moved to the Netherlands where, with Feyenoord he scored 42 goals in 149 appearances, winning two Dutch Cups (KNVB) in 1993/94 and 1994/95 and reaching the semi-finals of the European Cup Winners' Cup in 1995/96.

After sorting out contractual issues, Larsson was brought to Scotland by Wim Jansen, whom he had known from his time as Technical Director with Feyenoord. Over the next seven seasons, he would become known as the Super Swede, the Magnificent Seven (shirt number) and the King of Kings.

175 Scottish Premier League goals in 221 appearances, 242 goals in all competitions from 315 appearances. He is the third highest goalscorer in the history of Celtic FC, following Jimmy McGrory and Bobby Lennox, and 11 goals ahead of Stevie Chalmers.

With Celtic he won 4 Scottish Premier Leagues, 2 Scottish Cups, 2 Scottish League Cups. He was Scottish Footballer of the Year in 1998/99 and 2000/01. In the SPL he was top scorer five times: 1998/99 (29), 2000/01 (35), 2001/02 (29), 2002/03 (28), and 2003/04 (30).

In season 2000/01 he was the leading goalscorer in European club football, winning the European Golden Shoe (the new name since 1997 for the Golden Boot). In the SPL he scored 35 league goals, which UEFA deemed equivalent in Scotland of 35 x 1.5 = 52.5 bettering nearest rival Hernan Crespo of Lazio in Serie A, Italy 26 x 2 = 52.

Larsson and Celtic were good for each other!

In his first season, 1997/98, he scored in the League Cup Final victory over Dundee United. On the final day of the season versus St. Johnstone his goal helped to stop Rangers' 10 in a row march as Celtic won the league by two points.

After recovering from a broken leg in 1999, Larsson had a record breaking 2000/01 season. Celtic won the treble of SPL, Scottish Cup and Scottish League Cup, only the third Celtic side to do so, following the Jock Stein side of the 1960s. He scored 53 goals, the most since Charlie Nicholas' 50 in 1982/83. In the SPL he scored 35 league goals, the most by a Celtic player since the SPL formation in 1975/76 and equalling the league tally of Brian McClair from 1986/87.

The new 12 team 'split season' SPL was won, with Celtic champions after 38 games with 97 points, 15 points ahead of Rangers. He scored twice in the 3-0 Scottish Cup Final win versus Hibernian, after netting a brace in the semi-final versus Dundee United. In the Scottish League Cup, after another double in the semi-final versus Rangers he bagged a hat-trick in the final versus Kilmarnock.

He was crowned Scottish Footballer of the Year and was the top goalscorer throughout the European leagues. Manager Martin O'Neill enthused: "Henrik's as brave as a lion, a goal-getter, a truly great player, he would score goals in any league in any century."

The following season, 2001/02, the league was retained. In the 2002/03 campaign Larsson scored 11 goals in the UEFA Cup run as the Hoops reached their first European final since Celtic faced Feyenoord in the 1970 European Cup Final.

He scored in both 'Battle of Britain' ties versus Blackburn Rovers and Liverpool. In the semi-final versus Boavista he scored in both legs to see Celtic through 2-1 on aggregate.

In the final against José Mourinho's Porto in Seville he scored twice in a 3-2 defeat. "That was very hard to take. Winning a European trophy with Celtic would have meant so much to us and the fans. I still get goosebumps talking about it now."

2003/04 would be Larsson's final season with Celtic. The league was won and in his final league match at Parkhead he scored both goals in a 2-1 victory versus Dundee United. In his final competitive match, he scored twice again in the 3-1 win over Dunfermline Athletic in the Scottish Cup Final at Hampden Park.

In Old Firm encounters with Rangers, he is Celtic's post-war record scorer in the league with 11 goals, including doubles in the November 1998 (5-1) and August 2000 (6-2) victories.

When asked what was the weirdest thing ever tangled in his

dreadlocks, he answered, "Defenders!"

Larsson moved to Barcelona, scoring 22 goals in 62 appearances over two seasons. In 2004/05 Barca won La Liga for the first time since their centennial year of 1999. He returned to Parkhead, scoring in a 3-1 Barcelona victory in the Champions League in September 2004, cancelling out former strike partner Chris Sutton's Celtic equaliser.

In 2005/06, La Liga was retained and, coming on as a substitute in the Champions League Final versus Arsenal in 2006, he set up both goals to secure the cup 2-1. Arsenal's Thierry Henry. commenting, said, "Henrik Larsson had made the difference with his two assists."

In his career he scored 59 European club goals including a record 40 in the UEFA Cup/Europa League, with a club record 35 goals for Celtic in European competition.

After Barca he returned to Helsingborg, then had a highly influential short loan spell with Manchester United where he would have won a Premier League medal (but kept his promise to return to Helsingborg). He also played briefly in his homeland for Råå IF and his first club Högaborgs.

As Sweden's most well-known sportsperson, along with tennis champion Bjorn Borg, he has scored 37 goals in 106 internationals. At the 1994 World Cup in the USA he scored in the third place play-off win (4-0) versus Bulgaria. He also scored three goals at the 2002 World Cup finals and versus England in the 2-2 draw at the 2006 World Cup in Germany.

In the European Championships, he scored at Euro 2000 and was on target three times at Euro 2004 where he was named in the All-Star Team. In 2020 he returned to Barcelona as assistant to Ronald Koeman (the pair had played together at Feyenoord).

Henrik Larsson has never been afraid to stand up for 'right'. In 2016, he resigned as manager of Helsingborg after having to defend his playing son, Jordan, in a physical confrontation with 'supporters'. Showing no hard feelings, he returned to his home town club again in 2019. Affectionately he is known locally as 'Henke', referring to Helsingborg with encouraging words: "You must walk down to the beachfront before you leave." Sounds like paradise. Henrik Larsson knows all about that!

"Very soon after I came to Celtic, I realised how special the supporters are and they have been a big part of everything that has happened to me. I want them all to know their support has meant a great deal and is something I will never forget."

Ally McCoist

In post-war British football since 1945, Alistair Murdoch McCoist is the leading goalscorer for a single club in English and Scottish football.

355 league and cup goals for Glasgow Rangers in 581 appearances from

1983 to 1998. Super Ally was the first footballer on the continent to win the European Golden Boot since its inception in season 1967/68 in consecutive seasons, 1991/92 and 1992/93, with 34 league goals on both occasions.

McCoist was born in Bellshill, Lanarkshire, hailing from the same area as another all-time great goalscorer Hughie Gallacher, who preceded Coisty by some 60 years at the beginning of the 20th century.

As a youngster Alistair played for Calderwood Bluestar. When he was at High School he used to train with St. Mirren's Youth Team where manager Alex Ferguson would gave him a couple of quid for chips after sessions.

Although he was not picked up by Fergie, while playing for Fir Park Boys Club, he was signed by Jim Storrie at St. Johnstone. He made his debut for the Perth club in April 1979. In August 1980, just a month short of his eighteen birthday, he scored his first senior goal in a 3-0 win versus Dumbarton.

In that 1980/81 season he was the Scottish First Division leading scorer. In the summer of 1981, he became Sunderland's record signing for £400,000, after 22 league goals in 57 appearances for the Saints.

Manager Alan Durban gave Ally his English top-flight debut on the opening day of the 1981/82 season versus Ipswich Town. He scored his first goal versus Brian Clough's Nottingham Forest. His homesickness was eased by the company of his room mate at Sunderland, Frank Worthington, but after 8 league goals in 56 appearances he was offered the opportunity to return home.

"I met John Greig and Tommy McLean at the Crest Hotel at the roundabout in Carlisle. I went to a payphone and phoned my wee grannie in Thornliebank, first person I phoned. I can still hear her – obviously not with us now – but I can still her voice down the phone, I'm gonna sign for Rangers, you could have given her a million pounds and it wouldn't have meant just as much."

McCoist signed on the dotted line for £185,000 in June 1983. At the time Rangers were competing with Billy McNeill's Celtic, Alex Ferguson's Aberdeen and Jim McLean's Dundee United in an ultra-competitive Scottish Premier League. In September, on his debut, he scored after just 33 seconds at Parkhead in his first Old Firm derby in a 2-1 defeat to Celtic.

Even after such an encouraging start, he had a tough time early on at Ibrox, Ally admitting it 'made me stronger'. Jeers had turned to cheers by the time he had scored a hat-trick for new manager Jock Wallace in the League Cup final triumph over Celtic (3-2) in March 1984.

It was to be the first of a record nine League Cup winner's medals, with a competition record 54 goals. He also found the net in winning finals in October 1988 with a brace in a 3-2 win over Aberdeen. In October 1993 he came off the bench to score a spectacular overhead kick winner to defeat Hibernian 2-1 and in November 1996, two goals apiece from McCoist and Paul Gascoigne secured a ninth League Cup in a (4-3) Celtic Park thriller versus Hearts.

He was less fortunate in the Scottish Cup. He missed finals through injury and lost three of the four he played in. His winning final was in May 1992 versus Airdrie at Hampden Park, where Mark Hateley and Ally scored in a 2-1 win to bring the cup to Rangers for the first time in 11 years.

In the Scottish Premier League, his goalscoring ensured Rangers were once again the dominant force in Scottish football. In the 1986/87 season he scored 33 league goals as Rangers won their first Scottish league title since the 1977/78 season. Under player/manager Graeme Souness, Ally remembers: "We used to fight like cat and dog, was great for me, was absolutely great for me. Graeme Souness transformed Rangers FC and Scottish football."

In total McCoist won ten Scottish Premier League titles under Souness and Walter Smith including nine in a row from 1988/89 to 1996/97, equalling the Celtic record from 1965/66 to 1973/74.

He was the SPL top goalscorer three times – 1985/86 (24), 1991/92 (34) and 1992/93 (34). Sam English with 44 goals in 1931/32 holds the club record for league goals in season. Ally scored a club record 28 hat-tricks with a club record 27 goals in Old Firm games versus Celtic.

"I remember all the games vividly for one reason or another and the only thing that's constant is the atmosphere generated by the crowd. The game against Celtic is about noise, tension and passion. They are all must win, without exception and that will never change, regardless of who's in charge."

McCoist is Rangers' record league goalscorer with 251 league goals from 418 appearances, overtaking Bob McPhail on 233. The goals that made Ally Europe's top goalscorer in 1991/92 and 1992/93 also proved historically significant for Rangers, becoming the first Scottish club side to win the domestic treble in successive seasons. He was also the Scottish Footballer of the Year and PFA Player of the Year for 1991/92. In the 1992/93 season, he recorded a personal best 49 goals in league and cup from 52 appearances.

For Rangers in Europe, he scored 21 times. In the inaugural Champions League season of 1992/93, he memorably scored in both legs of the Battle of Britain Second Round tie versus the English champions Leeds United, a side containing Eric Cantona and Gary McAllister. Rangers were victorious over two legs (4-2) on aggregate and progressed to the group stage quarter-finals. In Group A, after six matches, Rangers finished unbeaten, runners-up to Marseille by a single point. With no semi-finals, the French club went on to defeat AC Milan in the final. In his playing career, this would be the closest Ally and Rangers would come to European glory.

McCoist's final season with Rangers was the 1997/98 campaign. In his last match he scored in the Scottish Cup Final defeat (2-1) to Hearts after he had also scored in the semi-final versus Celtic.

In August 1998, one month short of his 36th birthday, he joined former Ibrox team mate (now manager) Bobby Williamson at Kilmarnock. In October 1999, he suffered the second broken leg of his career during a 1-1 draw with Rangers. He played his final club match in May 2001, a 1-0 win versus Celtic that ensured Killie qualified for Europe. With Kilmarnock, McCoist scored 9 league goals in 53 appearances.

Ally is the record goalscorer in the history of the Scottish Premier League with 260 SPL goals. In total he has 290 English and Scottish league goals from 584 appearances, with a grand total of 405 club goals in all competitions.

At international level, he scored a further 19 in 61 Scotland appearances from 1986 to 1998. He scored his first goal in September 1987 with both goals in a 2-0 win versus Hungary at Hampden Park. In November 1989 versus Norway his goal secured Scotland the point they needed to qualify for a fifth consecutive World Cup (Italia '90) where he played all three group games. In March 1996 he captained his country for the only time and scored the only goal of the game versus Australia at Hampden. At Euro '96 he struck a stunning goal from outside the penalty box to defeat Switzerland (1-0) at Villa Park. He has also served his country as part of the coaching staff.

In 2007 he returned to Rangers as No.2 to Smith. In 2011 he became Rangers manager. In February 2012 the club were placed into administration and had to start at the bottom tier of the Scottish League. As manager, McCoist won the Third Division title in 2012/13 and the re-branded Scottish League One title in 2013/14, before resigning in

December 2014.

Ally is well known outside of football. From 1996 to 2007 he was a captain on *A Question of Sport*. In September 2000, the film *A Shot at Glory* starred Ally as the fictional former Celtic striker Jackie McQuillan, his coach was played by Hollywood screen icon Robert Duvall and it premiered at the Toronto Film Festival.

In January 2010, a sports centre in his home town of East Kilbride was renamed the Alistair McCoist Sports Complex. "I'm absolutely thrilled and very proud, the people of East Kilbride are a wonderful breed." Councillor Jim Docherty, a Celtic fan, said, "Ally has been a legend, not only for Rangers and Scotland, but for so many people in East Kilbride."

In 2021, as part of the ITV commentary team for Euro 2020, McCoist continues to be a man of the people, affable, engaging and entertaining as ever.

Michael Owen

"If I could relive one day from my career, the FA Cup Final of 2001 would be it." Michael Owen reflects on his favourite footballing moment when his two goals won Liverpool the cup underneath a sunshine sky at the Millennium Stadium, Cardiff. A goalscorer who dribbled past defenders to score wonder goals! The *Shoot!* magazine's 'Most Exciting Player Award' could have been invented for Michael. At his peak, electrifying quick, he won games on his 'Owen', before injuries robbed him off a yard or two of pace.

European Footballer of the Year for 2001, the first British player since Kevin Keegan in 1979 and the first British based since George Best in 1968 to be the recipient of the Ballon d'Or. Two-time Premier League Golden Boot winner in 1997/98 and 1998/99, the first teenager since Jimmy Greaves in 1958/59 to be top-flight leading scorer and the first teenager to do so in consecutive seasons since Tommy Lawton in 1937/38 and 1938/39.

He is one of only ten players with 150 or more Premier League goals and one of only six British footballers with 40 or more international goals. He is the youngest post-war English goalscoring captain and the first England player to score in four consecutive tournaments: World Cup '98, Euro 2000, World Cup 2002 and Euro 2004.

As a lad, Owen supported Everton, whom his dad Terry had played for. Aged eight he was already playing for Deeside Area Primary Schools Under-11 team. His mum, Jeanette, remembers Michael smashing the season goalscoring records of Ian Rush and Gary Speed's overall appearance record. Owen was born in Chester, the same year Rush made his league debut for the club and he would go on to break Rushie's Liverpool FC European goals record.

Whilst still attending the FA's School of Excellence at Lilleshall, Michael's goals won Liverpool their first ever FA Youth Cup in 1995/96. In the week of his 17th birthday in December 1996 he signed a professional contract with the Reds. In May 1997 he was given his league debut by Roy Evans, scoring versus Wimbledon at Selhurst Park to become the youngest ever goalscorer in the history of Liverpool Football Club at 17 years and 143 days.

At the start of the 1997/98 season, with regular penalty taker Robbie Fowler injured, Owen took responsibility from the spot on the opening day of the season and scored again versus Wimbledon.

In September, on his European debut, he scored versus Celtic at Parkhead. By the end of his first full season, he was voted PFA Young Player of the Year and was the Premier League top scorer with 18 league goals, shared with Dion Dublin and Chris Sutton. Among the 18, Owen became the youngest scorer of a Premier League hat-trick in February

1998 in the 3-3 draw away to Sheffield Wednesday, at 18 years 62 days. In the same month he became the youngest-ever player in the 20th century to make his debut for England at 18 years 59 days against Chile at Wembley. In May 1998, Owen also became England's youngest ever goalscorer at 18 years 5 months 13 days as a substitute for Ian Wright versus Morocco in Casablanca. Selected by Glenn Hoddle for the World Cup, he became an international superstar.

He scored in the group stage versus Romania and in St. Etienne in the Last 16 the nation was captivated by a Michael Owen wonder goal, gliding past the Argentinian defence. The game finished 2-2 and Michael scored in the penalty shoot-out, only for England to lose 4-3 on spot-kicks.

In August 1998, it was back to the league again, scoring an away day hat-trick versus Newcastle United. In October he hit four goals at Anfield versus Nottingham Forest. In December, Owen was voted BBC Sports Personality of the Year. In April 1999, Michael's hamstring give way, but he still had enough goals come the end of the season to be Premier League top scorer again with 18, shared with Jimmy Floyd Hasselbaink and Dwight Yorke.

In the calendar year of 2001, with Liverpool he won the League Cup, FA Cup, UEFA Cup, Charity Shield and UEFA Super Cup. In Europe he scored twice away to Roma. In the Premier League he scored a hat-trick at Anfield versus Newcastle, a double versus Chelsea and a goal at Charlton to ensure the Reds' Champions League qualification. In the FA Cup Final, with Liverpool playing in a change strip of yellow and blue, his two second half goals overturned an Arsenal lead in the first cup final at the Millennium Stadium, 'The Michael Owen Final'.

In August 2001, there was a Champions League hat-trick versus Haka and four days later a goal versus Manchester United in the Charity Shield and both goals on the opening day of the league season in a 2-1 victory versus West Ham United at Anfield. In the UEFA Super Cup Final in Monaco, he scored Liverpool's third in a 3-2 win versus Bayern Munich, "Michael Owen is a world class player and we simply could not counter his threat." – Bayern coach Ottmar Hitzfeld.

In September, on the Tuesday of the 9/11 New York twin towers attacks, Owen scored the Reds' first goal in the Champions League group stages in a 1-1 draw at Anfield versus Boavista. He also scored in the 3-1 Merseyside derby win versus Everton. For England he scored a hat-trick versus Germany (5-1) in Munich, with Liverpool team-mates Steven Gerrard and Emile Heskey also on target.

In November, he scored twice in the Premier League versus Manchester United (3-1) and against Barcelona in the Champions League. In December 2001, Owen was acclaimed as the finest footballer in Europe as the winner of the European Footballer of the Year. "We have had a great year at Liverpool, winning five trophies and I'm very happy to have won this award as well."

In the 2002/03 season, he scored a career best 28 league and cup goals. He scored in the League Cup Final win (2-1) versus Manchester United after also scoring the decisive goal in the semi-final versus Sheffield United at Anfield. In Europe there was a hat-trick away to Spartak Moscow. In the Premier League, a hat-trick versus Manchester City and in April 2003 a four-goal blast in a 6-0 away win versus West Brom with his second goal, his 100th in the Premier league, the youngest player to reach the century, aged 23 years 4 months 12 days.

The 2003/04 season would be Owen's final one on Merseyside, signing off as he started with a goal for the Reds in his last appearance versus Newcastle in May 2004. 118 Premier league goals in 216 appearances, 158 goals in all competitions from 297 Liverpool FC appearances. "Michael Owen scores the goals, Hallelujah!"

In the summer, as part of a deal involving Antonio Nunez going to Liverpool, he joined Real Madrid for £8m. As a 'Galactico' he scored 13 La Liga goals in 36 games, including in a 4-2 victory versus Barcelona as Real finished runners-up in the league.

Owen's heart was set on a return to Liverpool, but he ended up going to Newcastle for a club record £16m. Beset by injuries he only played 71 league games over four seasons, scoring 26 league goals, the highlights being a hat-trick playing alongside Alan Shearer versus West Ham in December 2005 and two goals in the Tyne-Wear derby versus Sunderland in April 2008.

In July 2009, to the dismay of all Liverpool supporters, Owen signed for Manchester United. He explained, "I left Newcastle and the first thing I did was to phone Carra and ask him to speak to the manager. However, at that time Liverpool wasn't an option, they didn't want me, so I signed for Man Utd." In three seasons at Old Trafford, Owen scored 5 Premier League goals from 31 games (25 as sub). In September 2009 he scored a late, late winner versus Manchester City (4-3). He grabbed another

Champions League hat-trick in December 2009 versus Wolfsburg. At Wembley, in the 2010 League Cup Final, he scored alongside Wayne Rooney in the victory over Aston Villa (2-1). In 2010/11 he was part of the squad that won the Premier League and was an unused substitute in the Champions League Final versus Barcelona.

In September 2012, Owen signed for Stoke City. He played eight Premier League games (all as substitute), scoring one goal. That single goal was away to Swansea City in January 2013 and was Michael's Owen's 150th and last in the Premier League. His Premier League record reads: 150 goals, 326 appearances. Overall he has 222 career club goals.

For England, after bursting onto the world stage at World Cup '98 he earned 89 England caps, scoring 40 international goals over ten years. Owen also scored at Euro 2000 versus Romania, World Cup 2002 versus Denmark and Brazil and Euro 2004 versus Portugal, where he also scored in a penalty shoot-out (losing 6-5 on spot-kicks). He also played at the 2006 World Cup in Germany. He also scored twice versus Argentina in 3-2 friendly win in November 2005 in Geneva. Owen captained his country eight times.

He made his final professional appearance in May 2013 in a 1-1 draw for Stoke City versus Southampton at the St. Mary's Stadium, with both sets of fans chanting his name and receiving a standing ovation from all four corners of the ground at the final whistle.

Owen has since had a successful career in the media and as a breeder of racehorses, including Brown Panther. He also climbed into the saddle, riding Calder Prince to second place in a charity race at Ascot in 2017.

In 2020, on Jamie's Carragher's podcast *The Greatest Game*, Michael opened up on his leaving of Liverpool and subsequent move to Manchester United and Liverpool fans' reaction, "It has killed me for ages and the wound will never go. I know who my club is, but I can't change what I have done, I made the decision, I am not blaming anyone, I still love Liverpool."

Wayne Rooney

England's all-time top goalscorer, Manchester United's all-time top goalscorer, eclipsing Bobby Charlton's long-standing records at both international and club level.

Wayne Rooney set new goalscoring landmarks playing the game with a freedom of expression. A 21st century force of nature. Perhaps 'the last of the street footballers'.

An unselfish goalscorer who would accommodate team mates, play out wide and drop back into midfield. Injuries and suspensions (he was red carded six times in his career) have been a by-product of his willingness to constantly contribute, to benefit the team, coupled with a fierce natural exuberance to always be at the centre of the action. In the first two decades of the new millennium, 18 seasons of total commitment. 313 career club goals from 763 appearances for Everton, Manchester United, DC United and Derby County. 53 international goals from 120 caps.

Wayne Rooney just loves playing football! With Manchester United he has won five Premier League titles: 2006/07, 2007/08, 2008/09, 2010/11, 2012/13; a Champions League in 2008; a Europa League in 2017; the FA Cup in 2016; three League Cups, 2006, 2010, 2017; and a Club World Cup in 2008. In 2009/10 he was voted Footballer of the Year and PFA Young Player of the Year and PFA Player of the Year in 2004/05 and 2005/06.

Rooney is the most recent member and one of only 29 players in the history of English football with 200 or more top-flight league goals. His 208 Premier League goals from 491 appearances also make him the second highest goalscorer in Premier League history. He is also the only player with more than 200 top-flight league goals to make over 100 assists.

A bread and butter Scouser from Croxeth, Liverpool, he played for Copplehouse Under-10s. While training at Liverpool FC Juniors he still wore his Everton kit. He was scouted by Bob Pendleton and signed to the Everton Academy. His hero growing up was the Blues' Number 9 Duncan Ferguson. In November 1995 he was the Everton mascot in the Merseyside derby at Anfield and when he scored in the FA Youth Cup Final versus Aston Villa he revealed a T-shirt: "Once a Blue, always a Blue."

In August 2002 he was given his first team debut by David Moyes in the 2-2 home draw with Spurs. In October he scored his first senior goals for Everton in the League Cup away to Wrexham. Later in the month, five days before his 17th birthday, he became the youngest goalscorer in Premier League history with a spectacular long-range last-minute winner to end Arsenal's 30 match unbeaten run. "The greatest young English talent I have ever seen." – Gunners' manager Arsène Wenger. "Remember the name – Wayne Rooney." – Commentator Clive Tyldesley.

Less than four months later he made his England international debut at Upton Park versus Australia in February 2003 as England's youngest player, aged 17 years 111 days. In September 2003 he became his nation's youngest ever goalscorer aged 17 years 317 days in a European Championship qualifier versus Macedonia in Skopje.

At Euro 2004 he set the tournament alight. He scored four goals, twice in both games versus Switzerland (3-0) and Croatia (4-2). In the quarter-final versus hosts Portugal he broke a bone in his foot and England lost the penalty shoot-out 6-5. He was a revelation and was selected in the Team of the Tournament.

By the start of the new Premier League season, Rooney was a United player. After 15 league goals in 67 Everton appearances, he became the world's most expensive teenage footballer, signing for Alex Ferguson's Manchester United in August 2004 for £26.6m. The following month he netted a wonderful hat-trick on his United debut in a Champions League tie with Fenerbahçe at Old Trafford, with Denis Law enthusing, "Every time he got the ball, there was a buzz of expectation from the crowd... Rooney can do the lot, eventually he'll have all the United records."

Rooney's first silverware with United was the 2006 League Cup. He scored twice in Cardiff in a 4-0 win over Wigan Athletic. In the 2006/07 season he scored twice versus AC Milan in the Old Trafford, Champions League 1st leg semi-final, but lost out on aggregate (5-3). He won his first Premier League title, netting in total 23 goals in all competitions.

In the 2007/08 season, alongside Cristiano Ronaldo and Carlos Tevez, United won the Premier League and Champions League double, denying Chelsea at home and in the penalty shoot-out in Moscow.

In December 2008 he won the Golden Ball as the best player of the tournament at the FIFA Club World Cup. In Japan he scored twice in the semi-final versus Gamba Osaka and the winning goal in the final against Liga de Quito in Yokohama. In the second half of the 2008/09 season, United lost in the final of the Champions League in Rome to Barcelona. The Premier League was retained with Rooney scoring the vital two goals in a comeback win over Spurs at Old Trafford in April to hold off nearest challengers Liverpool.

In the 2009/10 season he scored 34 goals in all competitions, with 26 in the Premier League, including all four versus Hull City in January 2010. He scored five in Europe in games versus Bayern Munich and AC Milan. In the League Cup he scored in the semi-final aggregate victory over Manchester City (4-3) and in the final triumph (2-1) versus Aston Villa.

In October 2010, Rooney announced his intention to leave United, but in a dramatic change of heart stayed at Old Trafford and drove United onto a record-breaking 19th top-flight league title, the highlight being an overhead bicycle kick versus Man City in February 2011. "We've had some fantastic goals here, but in terms of execution, you'll never see that! It was unbelievable." – Alex Ferguson. Rooney also scored a hat-trick at West Ham after United were two-nil down and a penalty at Blackburn Rovers to secure the point to capture another Premier League crown. In the Champions League he scored in the semi-final versus Schalke 04 and scored again in the final at Wembley in the 3-1 defeat to Barcelona.

In 2011/12 he scored a career high 27 Premier League goals including back-to-back hat-tricks versus Arsenal (8-2) and away to Bolton (5-0). He also scored the winner at Sunderland on the final day of the season, but the Premier League title went to 'noisy neighbours' Manchester City on goal difference.

In Alex Ferguson's final season as manager in 2012/13, the Premier League was regained, for a record 20th top-flight championship, Rooney scoring twice in a 3-2 away win at City.

Over the next four seasons he had three managers, David Moyes, Louis van Gaal and José Mourinho. Having been made captain by van Gaal, he finally won the FA Cup (after losing finals in 2005 and 2007), lifting the trophy in 2016 after beating Crystal Palace 2-1 after extra time.

In his final season, 2016/17 under Mourinho, as club captain he lifted the League Cup as an unused substitute in February 2017 after victory versus Southampton (3-2).

In April 2017 he scored his final goal at Old Trafford, a penalty in a 1-1 draw with Swansea City. In May, in Stockholm, he made his final United appearance as a late substitute in the Europa League Final 2-0 win against Ajax.

The Lawman's prophecy came to pass, threefold: In the history of Manchester United, Rooney is the club's record goalscorer with 253 goals in all competitions from 559 appearances. The leading United goalscorer in the Premier league with 183 goals from 393 appearances and a club record 39 European goals.

In August 2017 he scored on his second Premier League debut for Everton in a 1-0 home win versus Stoke City. In November 2017, a month after his 32nd birthday, he hit a hat-trick at Goodison Park in a 4-0 win versus West Ham, the third goal a stunning strike from inside his own half. In two spells with Everton, he scored 25 league goals in 98 appearances.

In June 2018 he signed for MLS side DC United in Washington DC, scoring 25 goals in 52 games. In August 2019 he joined Derby County of the Championship as player/coach. In January 2021 he was appointed the club's new manager. His final professional appearance was for Derby away to Middlesbrough in November 2019.

For England, after Euro 2004 he played in a further five finals: 2006 World Cup, 2010 World Cup, 2012 Euros, scoring versus Ukraine and in the penalty shoot-out quarter-final defeat to Italy. He also scored at the 2014 World Cup versus Uruguay and in the Euro 2016 defeat to Iceland. He captained his country 22 times and also scored international goals versus Argentina, Holland, Brazil and France. In September 2015, in a European Championship qualifier, his successful penalty versus Switzerland saw him became the first British footballer to score 50 goals in international football.

In 2016 his testimonial match raised £1.2m for good causes. Recognising his own journey to give something back, the Wayne Rooney Foundation events contribute vital funds and support to charitable organisations including the NSPCC and the Alder Hey Children's Hospital.

Like in his playing days, an enthusiastic giver. "Roon-ey! Roon-ey!"

Alan Shearer

The Premier League record scorer with 260 goals, the fastest player to 100 Premier League goals in 124 games, three Premier League Golden Boots, a record seven seasons of 20 or more Premier League goals, a record 56 Premier League penalties.

The status of Alan Shearer as a legendary goalscorer is not confined to the Premier League alone. In the history of English top-flight football, dating back to the inaugural 1888/89 season, Shearer is 5th on the all-time top-flight goalscorers list with 283 league goals.

Shearer: the first since Rush to score 30 top-flight goals in two seasons, the first since Lineker to be top scorer in three seasons. Along with Jimmy Greaves and David Jack, he is one of only three players to have scored 100 or more top-flight league goals for two separate clubs. Shearer: the first since Greaves to be top scorer in three successive seasons: 1994/95 (34), 1995/96 (31) and 1996/97 (25). Indeed, he achieved something that the incomparable Greaves did not, scoring 30 English top-flight goals in three successive seasons: 1993/94 (31), 1994/95 (34) and 1995/96 (31). We have to go back to the 1920s to David Halliday's run of four successive seasons of 30 plus English top-flight goals for Sunderland to measure Shearer's accomplishment. For the record, Greaves scored 30 or more top-flight goals in four successive seasons, with one season in Italy and England. Shearer is a modern-day goal-machine among the all-time greats of goalscoring.

He is from the Gosforth area of Newcastle-Upon-Tyne. Playing for Wallsend Boys Club in Newcastle, he was spotted by Southampton FC scout Jack Hixen. He joined up with the Saints' youth team, renowned for bringing young players through.

In the spring of 1988, after a couple of substitute appearances, he was given his full debut by manager Chris Nicholl. In the First Division match versus Arsenal at The Dell on 9th April he became the youngest player to score a top-flight hat-trick (aged 17 years 240 days), beating the previous record held by Jimmy Greaves. He took the match ball home to his digs and the following day after his historic treble was back at the ground to clean the kit and players boots. "Looking back, it was a great thing to do," remembers Shearer. After such an explosive start, the young Shearer made steady progress over the next few seasons. In 1991 he was the competition top scorer as England won the Under-21 Toulon tournament.

In the final season of the First Division pre-Premier League football (1991/92), he scored 13 league goals. In February 1992 he made his England debut under Graham Taylor, scoring with Lineker in the friendly win versus France at Wembley. He was selected for the Euro '92 squad and played in the goalless game versus France.

In the summer of 1992, after 23 league goals in 118 appearances for the Saints, the one-time £35 a week YTS lad became British football's most expensive footballer, joining newly promoted Blackburn Rovers for £3.6m, convinced of the potential of the club by benevolent owner Jack Walker and the management team of Kenny Dalglish and Ray Harford.

On the opening weekend of the first Premier League season, he scored twice on his debut in a 3-3 draw at Selhurst Park versus Crystal Palace. In his first home match at Ewood Park he scored the only goal of the game to defeat Arsenal. In October he scored a brace in a 7-1 win over Norwich City. On Boxing Day, he had scored twice versus Leeds United to take his tally to 16 goals from 21 Premier League games, then in the last ten minutes he suffered a cruciate ligament injury, ruling him out for the rest of the season.

Recovered for the 1993/94 season, he scored 31 Premier League goals. He scored a hat-trick at Elland Road versus Leeds (3-3), both goals in a 2-0 victory over Southampton and again both goals in April versus title rivals Manchester United. Blackburn finished the season as runners-up to United, with Shearer voted Footballer of the Year, the first Rovers player to win the award.

In season 1994/95, he was PFA Player of the Year and Premier League and overall league top scorer with a personal best of 34 top-flight goals. In an ever-present season his goals in partnership with Chris Sutton ('SAS'), the dream became a reality as Blackburn Rovers were crowned English Champions for the first time in 81 years since the 1913/14 season.

Alan praised the team spirit created by Kenny Dalglish and the contribution of his team mates, in particular the supply line of old-fashioned wingers Stuart Ripley and Jason Wilcox. He scored three hat-tricks against QPR (4-0), West Ham (4-2) and Ipswich (4-1). He scored the only goal in the final home game of the season versus Newcastle. At Anfield in May, in the season finale, he opened the scoring versus Liverpool, who then won 2-1, but with West Ham holding Man Utd at Upton Park, Rovers were champions! "West Ham did us a great favour, so we got over the line in the end. It was brilliant, it was a huge relief. There were great scenes in the dressing room after the game and ones that I will never forget."

"Alan is a player in a class of his own, he lifts the whole team and turns draws into victories. In a word, priceless." – Kenny Dalglish

In 1995/96, Shearer was again the country's top goalscorer. In 35 Premier League appearances he scored 31 of Blackburn's 61 Premier League goals as Rovers finished seventh. He scored a record five hat-tricks, against Coventry (5-1), Forest (7-0), West Ham (4-2), Bolton (3-1) and away to Spurs (3-2).

At Euro '96, the summer that saw 'Football Coming Home', Shearer scored in all three group games versus Switzerland (1-1), Scotland (2-0) and twice versus Holland (4-1). In the quarter-final versus Spain, he scored in the penalty shoot-out (4-2) after the game ended goalless. In the Wembley semi-final versus Germany, he scored in the 1-1 draw and again in the shoot-out, as England lost 6-5 on penalties.

Shearer finished the tournament as top scorer with five goals. "Once we got knocked out of Euro '96, I had phone calls left, right and centre, Man Utd wanted me, so did Newcastle." Shearer made his mind up; he was going home. In four seasons with Blackburn he scored 112 Premier League goals in 138 appearances. He joined Newcastle for a world record £15m. "For me, as a player from the area, it was always my dream. I used to go and stand on the terraces as a 12-year-old to watch my hero Kevin Keegan. Now he was my manager."

In his first season on Tyneside, he was voted the PFA Player of the Year for a second time and was the Premier League top scorer for a third successive season with 25 goals as Newcastle finished runners-up. He scored versus Blackburn (2-1), in the Tyne-Wear derby versus Sunderland (1-1) and against Man Utd (5-0), two goals versus Spurs in a 7-1 win and a hat-trick against Leicester. After Keegan departed, Terry McDermott (caretaker) and Kenny Dalglish were in charge at St. James Park.

In the pre-season prior to the start of the 1997/98 season he suffered another serious injury, this time to his ankle. He again fought back to fitness and returned to score the winner versus Sheffield United in the semi-final of the FA Cup at Old Trafford. In the final, Newcastle lost to double winners Arsenal.

In the 1998/99 season Shearer scored both goals in the FA Cup semi-final to return Newcastle to Wembley, but again the final was lost, this time to treble chasing Man Utd.

In 1999/2000, after being left out of the Tyne-Wear derby by manager Ruud Gullit, normal service was restored when, in new manager Bobby Robson's first game in charge in September 1999, Shearer hit five goals in an 8-0 win over Sheffield Wednesday. The same month he scored his only England hat-trick in a 6-0 European

Championship qualifier versus Luxembourg at Wembley.

Before Euro 2000, Shearer had in advance indicated that he would be retiring from international football. With Kevin Keegan as England manager Shearer scored in the 3-2 defeat versus Romania. Versus Germany in Charleroi, Belgium, he scored the only goal of the game to give England their first competitive victory over their old rivals since the 1966 World Cup Final. With seven Euros goals, he is third on the all-time list behind Ronaldo and Platini. In total he scored 30 international goals in 63 games, 34 as captain.

In the 2001/02 and 2002/03 seasons, Shearer scored 40 Premier League goals as Newcastle finished fourth and third in the table. In 2003/04 he scored 22 Premier League goals and was the joint top scorer along with Didier Drogba of Marseille with six, as Newcastle reached the semi-finals of the UEFA Cup.

In 2004/05 he was set to retire at the end of the season but was encouraged by manager Graeme Souness to play on. In 2005/06, with Glenn Roeder in charge, Shearer broke Jackie Milburn's club goalscoring record. In April 2006, with three league games of the season remaining, he scored in his final Tyne-Wear derby versus Sunderland in a 4-1 victory, injuring his left knee. "Deep down I knew when I limped out of the Stadium of Light that was probably the end, and I the think the fans knew it as well." Just a couple of days earlier he had scored twice in a 3-1 victory against Wigan, which turned out to be his final appearance at St. James Park.

In 303 Premier League appearances for Newcastle he scored 148 goals, with 206 goals in all competitions. Premier League record: 260 goals in 441 games. Top-flight record: 283 goals in 559 games. In total, 379 career club goals.

Since retiring he has worked with the BBC as an analyst. In 2008/09 season, he managed Newcastle for the final eight league games of the season, with the club destined for relegation.

In 2012 he launched the Alan Shearer Foundation, fundraising for charitable good causes. In 2016 he attended the unveiling of the Alan Shearer statue at St. James Park. "I'm very proud, very honoured... because after all I got paid to play football, I got paid to score goals, so I was one lucky boy."

In 2021, Shearer was among the first two inductees into the Premier League Hall of Fame. Thanking team mates, coaches and managers he said, "All I ever wanted was to be a professional footballer. It was a dream to do that. I enjoyed every minute of it."

Jamie Vardy

When the legend is fact and not a myth, reality provides a wonderful landscape. The Jamie Vardy story is a portrait of a footballer that goes beyond the imagination of any fictional creation.

A dream catcher from the character-building platform of non-league football to a history maker with Leicester City Football Club and England international.

Premier League Champion, FA Cup winner, Footballer of the Year and Golden Boot winner. Jamie and Leicester achieved immortality by winning the Premier League (the club's first top-flight title) in 2015/16 and the FA Cup in 2021 for the first time in 137 years of club history.

Vardy's journey began in his hometown of Sheffield. A trainee with Wednesday, he was released for being too small. "I wasn't physically built enough. It does hit you hard, I was very angry and upset and that is why I stopped playing for a year."

He returned to the game with Stocksbridge Park Steels of the Northern Premier League, playing for the Under-18s and reserves. Moving up to the first team in 2007, he scored 66 goals in 107 appearances. In 2010 he was transferred for £15,000 to FC Halifax Town, scoring 29 goals in 41 appearances. Vardy then joined National League side Fleetwood Town for the significant fee of £150,000.

Continuing his football with his part-time employment in a factory, in season 2011/12 he scored 34 goals in 42 appearances, 31 in the league as Town were promoted to the Football League for the first time in club history. He also scored three times in an FA Cup run that saw the north-west club reach the 3rd round proper for the first time ever. In May 2012, for a non-league record of £1 (rising to £1.7m with add-ons), he was transferred to Championship side, Leicester City.

He made a goalscoring debut versus Torquay United in a 4-0 win at Plainmoor in the 1st round of the League Cup. His Football league debut was at home to Peterborough United in a 2-1 home win and, aged 25, he scored his first goal in the Football League in August 2012 in a 2-1 defeat to Blackburn Rovers at Ewood Park.

Leicester finished the season in 6th place, above Bolton on goal difference, qualifying for the play-offs. In the semi-final versus Watford, Jamie and team-mate Harry Kane (on loan from Spurs) were both on the bench in the second leg, as Leicester lost out 3-2 on aggregate.

In his first season of league football, he had scored five goals in all competitions. Struggling in a new environment, "I had a chat with Nigel

Pearson… trying to get him to loan me back to Fleetwood, just because I'd had success there." Encouraged by manager Pearson that he was good enough "you can play a lot higher", after that it all clicked together.

In 2013/14, Vardy scored 16 league goals, including versus promotion rivals, away to QPR (1-0) and at home to Derby County (4-1). In partnership with David Nugent, Leicester won the Championship by nine points from Burnley, returning to the Premier League for the first time since 2003/04.

In August 2014, aged 27, Vardy made his Premier League top-flight debut in a 1-1 draw with Arsenal. The following month, he scored his first Premier League goal in the memorable 5-3 victory over Manchester United at the KP Stadium.

By the spring, Leicester were bottom of the Premier League with nine games to go, then began 'The Great Escape', winning seven and drawing one of their remaining league fixtures. Vardy scored crucial goals during the run in, including a last-minute winner at the Hawthorns versus West Brom (3-2) and the only goal of the game at Turf Moor versus Burnley to lift the Foxes out of the relegation zone. Now safe, he also scored in the last league game of the season in a 5-1 victory versus QPR.

In 2015/16, under the management of Claudio Ranieri, Vardy scored Leicester's first goal of the new season, in an opening day win versus Sunderland (4-2). At the end of the month (August) he scored a late penalty equaliser away to Bournemouth. It was to signal the start of a record-breaking run of scoring in eleven consecutive Premier League games (13 goals). In game number ten he equalled Ruud Van Nistelrooy's Premier League record with a goal in the 3-0 away win at Newcastle. The next match he scored in the 1-1 home draw with Manchester United to equal Stan Mortensen's post-war top-flight record from the 1950/51 First Division season with Blackpool FC.

Leicester's title challenge built momentum. In December, Vardy scored in a 2-1 victory over champions Chelsea. In February, he scored both goals in a 2-0 win versus Liverpool, establishing a three-point lead over Manchester City after 24 Premier League matches, Jurgen Klopp describing Jamie's opener as "world class".

In April he scored twice in a 2-0 away win at Sunderland, for Leicester to go seven points clear of Spurs with five games to go.

In May, as Spurs drew with Chelsea, Leicester City were confirmed as Premier League champions. In the final home game of the season, on

Saturday 7th May 2016, the Fantastic Mr Foxes were presented with the Premier League trophy after the match. In the 3-1 victory over Everton, Jamie scored his 23rd and 24th Premier League goals of the season. He was also voted Footballer of the Year, the first Leicester City player to win the award.

Premier League champions by ten points from Arsenal, with only 3 league defeats all season and a club record 23 top-flight wins, Leicester became the first maiden winners of the English top-flight since Brian Clough's Nottingham Forest in 1977/78.

During the summer transfer window, Arsenal triggered a release clause in Jamie's contract, bidding £20m plus. "Every time I thought about it, my heart and head were coming to the same answer, which was to stay."

Vardy began the 2016/17 season as a Leicester player. In August, he scored in the Charity Shield defeat to Manchester United. In December 2016 he scored his first Premier League hat-trick versus Manchester City in a 4-2 win at the King Power Stadium. In Europe, Leicester topped their Champions League group to quality for the knockout stage. By February, Leicester had sacked their title-winning manager Claudio Ranieri, replaced by Craig Shakespeare. In the Premier League, Vardy scored twice in a 3-1 win versus Liverpool. In Europe, in the Round of 16, he scored in the 1st leg 2-1 away defeat to Sevilla with Leicester prevailing 3-2 on aggregate. In the quarter-finals he again found the net against Spanish opposition with a goal in the 1-1 home draw to Atletico Madrid with Leicester exiting the Champions League 2-1 on aggregate.

In seasons 2017/18 and 2018/19 Vardy scored 20 and 18 Premier League goals respectively and faced his old side Fleetwood in the Third Round of the FA Cup in January 2018.

In 2019/20 he won the Premier League Golden Boot with 23 goals, the first Leicester City player since Gary Lineker in 1984/85 to be the leading goalscorer in England's top flight. With Brendan Rodgers now manager, his total included a goalscoring run of 11 goals in 8 consecutive games, including a hat-trick in a record top-flight away victory of 9-0 at the St. Mary's Stadium versus Southampton in October 2019.

In 2020/21 he scored his third Premier League hat-trick in a 5-2 away win at Manchester City. In the FA Cup, Leicester reached their first semi-final since 1982, beating Southampton 1-0. In their first final since 1969, the Foxes beat Chelsea to win the cup for the first time in club history in their fifth FA Cup Final.

A week later at the King Power, Vardy scored two penalties in 4-2 home defeat to Spurs, as Leicester missed out on Champions League qualification by a point. After the match the FA Cup was paraded around the ground.

Vardy has scored 42 Premier League goals against the so-called 'Top Six', with manager Rodgers saying, "Jamie is irreplaceable."

At international level, his rise is just as remarkable. He made his England bow, capped by Roy Hodgson in June 2015 as a substitute for Wayne Rooney versus the Republic of Ireland in Dublin.

He scored his first international goal, up front with Kane in March 2016 in a 3-2 win versus Germany in Berlin. At Euro 2016 he scored the opener in the 2-1 win against Wales. In March 2018 at Wembley in a pre-World Cup friendly he scored in a 1-1 draw with Italy (when VAR was used for the first time in an England match). Gareth Southgate selected him in his World Cup squad for Russia and he played in four games, including as a substitute in the semi-final defeat to Croatia. In total Jamie scored 7 international goals, including against Holland and Spain in 26 appearances.

Eight years on from being on the bench in the Championship play-offs: Jamie Vardy, Premier League champion, Footballer of the Year, World Cup semi-finalist, Golden Boot winner, FA Cup winner and Community Shield winner.

In June 2021, Vardy posted on his Twitter and Instagram accounts that he was to become a co-owner of the American football club the Rochester Rhinos. "I also can't thank Leicester City Football Club enough for allowing me to do this, they know, and I know, that this project will not in any way distract me from my priority, which is helping Leicester to be successful for many more years to come."

All followers of Leicester City say amen to that. 150 goals, with 121 Premier league goals in 250 games. The Jamie Vardy Story continues... Hollywood should make a movie!

Ian Wright

Ian Wright's appreciative fulfilment at being a professional footballer is a reflection of a hard knocks background.

A teenager with a criminal record, "I was an angry young man, I didn't have the best of role models early on, so like a lot of kids in South London, I played football every chance I got." (Usually at the park, called Hilly Fields.)

As in life, football is all about who you meet on the way. While attending Turnham Junior School in Brockley, South London, teacher Sydney Pigden had a positive influence on the young Ian, teaching him how to read and write and social development skills. Mr Pigden also recognised and encouraged his football, "Not to blast the ball, but pass it into the net, like Jimmy Greaves. Ever since then, I always tried to score with precision, not power."

Playing Sunday League football, Wright had various jobs including bricklayer and in maintenance in the Tunnel Refineries factory. He had trials with Charlton, Millwall and Brighton, but was rejected by all three clubs.

Crystal Palace scout Peter Prentice recommended Ian. "Thank the big man above that Crystal Palace saw something in me, because to do that trial, I had to take two weeks off my well-paid job that was supporting my young family." In August 1985, Palace bought Wright from Greenwich Borough for £200 in gym equipment.

By the end of the month, he had made his Football League debut versus Huddersfield Town. In October, a month before his 22nd birthday, he scored his first league goal. Described in the newspapers as 'a virtual unknown', he came on as a substitute for Trevor Aylott, scoring a last-minute winner (3-2) versus Oldham Athletic.

Manager Steve Coppell commented, "Ian injured himself celebrating the goal, I think he tried to jump over the stand, three months ago he was playing Sunday league football."

In season 1987/88 he scored 20 league goals as Palace finished 6th in the Second Division, unfortunate to miss out on the play-offs (contested that season between the 3rd, 4th and 5th placed sides in the Second Division and the 18th placed side in the 21 club, for that season, First Division).

The following season, 1988/89, he scored 33 goals, including 24 in the league. Palace finished third behind Chelsea and Manchester City to make the play-offs. In the semi-finals Wright, along with strike partner

Mark Bright, scored a goal apiece in the second leg home match to beat Swindon Town 2-1 on aggregate. In the two-legged, home and away play-off final versus Blackburn Rovers, after losing the first match 3-1, Ian scored twice, including an extra-time winner to see the Eagles promoted 4-3 on aggregate.

In his first season in the top flight he was restricted by injuries, which caused him to miss Palace's FA Cup semi-final victory over Liverpool. In the club's first ever FA Cup Final in May 1990, Ian came off the bench to score twice in a 3-3 extra time draw with Manchester United. "I felt I was welling up, this was the greatest moment of my life." The following Thursday United won the replay 1-0.

In the 1990/91 season, Wright scored 25 goals including a hat-trick in Palace's record cup victory, 8-0 versus Southend United in the League Cup Second Round in September 1990. In the league his 15 goals helped Palace achieve the club's highest ever league position of third, behind Arsenal and Liverpool. In the final two league games of the season, he scored an away day hat-trick at Wimbledon and a goal in a 3-0 victory versus Manchester United. Returning to Wembley he again scored twice in the Full Members Cup Final as Palace beat Everton 4-1.

In September 1991, he was signed by the champions Arsenal, managed by George Graham, for a club record £2.5m. Having already scored five league goals in the new league season for Palace, in total Ian scored 117 goals for the Selhurst Park club, including 89 league goals in 225 league appearances.

Woolwich born Ian made his debut for the Arsenal in the League Cup, scoring away at Leicester City. He hit a hat-trick on his league debut in a 4-0 victory at Southampton and also hit four versus Everton 4-2 and found the net in both North London derbies versus Spurs.

In May 1992, in the last ever game of the North Bank Terrace at Highbury he scored another hat-trick versus the Saints in a 5-1 win, including two late goals to finish the season with 24 Arsenal league goals, along with his 5 earlier in the season for Palace, to take his tally to 29 league goals to pip Spurs' Gary Lineker to the First Division Golden Boot. In doing so, he became the first player to be leading scorer in the top flight of English football, playing and scoring for two separate clubs in the same season. He was also top scorer in the Football League for season 1991/92.

In 1992/93 he scored in both League Cup semi-final legs versus former club Palace in a 5-1 aggregate victory, with the final won 2-1 versus Sheffield Wednesday. In the FA Cup Final he scored in the 1-1 draw with Wednesday and again in the replay, to take his total to 30 goals for the season and 10 in the FA Cup as Arsenal won the cup 2-1 to become the first side to lift both domestic cups in the same season. It was also the first FA Cup Final where players had their names on the backs of their shirts. With Wright scoring and being on the winning side, he emulated the great Dixie Dean, 60 years earlier in 1933 in the first cup final where players had numbers on the back of their shirts.

He scored a personal best 35 goals, including 23 in the Premier League in season 1993/94, again in both North London derbies and a third hat-trick versus Southampton. In the European Cup Winners' Cup, Arsenal reached their first European final since the Brady and Jennings side of 1980. Wright missed the final in Copenhagen through suspension after having scored a vital semi-final away goal against Paris St. Germain. Arsenal won their first European trophy since 1970, beating the Italians Parma.

He topped the 30-goal mark again in 1994/95, scoring in 12 consecutive appearances in all competitions (16 goals) between September and November. In Europe in the spring, he scored in both legs of the semi-finals of the Cup Winners' Cup versus Sampdoria, with the tie ending 5-5 on aggregate, Arsenal going through 3-2 on penalties. Between the European games he a scored a hat-trick versus Ipswich, 4-1 in the Premier League. The final in Paris was then lost to Real Zaragoza 2-1.

In season 1996/97 he scored another 23 Premier League goals including in a (20 club season) against a record 17 of the 19 competing clubs, with a hat-trick versus Sheffield Wednesday and both goals in a 2-0 win at Blackburn Rovers in Arsène Wenger's first match in charge.

In Wrighty's final season with Arsenal in 1997/98 he scored a hat-trick in September versus Bolton at Highbury to become the club's record scorer, overtaking Cliff Bastin's total of 178 goals.

In October, a month before his 34th birthday, he scored his final goal at Highbury in a 5-0 win versus Barnsley. His final Arsenal goal was away to West Ham United in the quarter-finals of the League Cup in a 2-1 win at Upton Park in January 1998.

Hampered by injuries and the Bergkamp/Anelka partnership, he was an unused substitute as Arsenal won the FA Cup Final versus Newcastle. His final Highbury appearance was versus Everton in May 1998 with Arsenal clinching the Premier League title on the day.

Ian Wright, Arsenal Record: 128 league goals in 221 appearances. 104

Premier League goals in 191 appearances. 185 goals in all competitions from 288 games.

Moving to West Ham United he scored 9 Premier League goals in 22 appearances during the 1998/99 season, including on his debut versus Sheffield Wednesday and at White Hart Lane against a Spurs side managed by George Graham.

He then had a loan spell with Nottingham Forest in the Championship under former Arsenal and England team-mate David Platt netting 5 league goals in 10 appearances, scoring again on debut versus QPR at the City Ground in a 1-1 draw in August 1999.

There then followed a move to Celtic as a replacement for the injured Henrik Larsson, scoring on debut in the SPL versus Kilmarnock 5-1. At Parkhead his record was 3 league goals in 8 appearances, before joining his final club Burnley in the third tier (Second Division) in February 2000. He scored 4 league goals in 15 appearances, including versus Reading, managed by his old Palace team-mate Alan Pardew. His final game as a professional was on the last day of the season as Burnley won promotion with a 2-1 win at Scunthorpe. "It was a great way for me to sign off."

Six clubs: 238 league goals in 501 appearances. 113 Premier League goals in 213 PL appearances. 324 goals in all competitions including one in the 1993 Charity Shield.

At international level, he scored 9 for England in 33 caps. He was given his first cap as a Palace player by Graham Taylor in a 2-0 Wembley win versus Cameroon in February 1991. His first goal was in a World Cup qualifier away to Poland in May 1993. In November 1993 he scored four away to San Marino (7-1) and also scored versus Italy in the Tournoi de France in June 1997.

In the 1990's Wrighty was featured in a Nike Billboard campaign: "Behind every great goalkeeper there's a ball from Ian Wright." He was responsible for giving supporters of Crystal Palace and Arsenal that feeling of joyful emotion more often than not, through club songs "Glad All Over" and "One Nil to the Arsenal".

In September 2021, Ian's first children's book, *Striking Out*, was inspired by his own story.

As Wrighty said, his journey to the top wasn't your typical one. "Woolwich born, Brockley bred, raised in Crystal Palace and grown by the Arsenal FC family. I'm proud of that mix; it made me the footballer I finally became, and the man, father and football pundit I am today."

Goals Encore

The greatest hits from our greatest goalscorers. As with any 'best of' collection, whether that be football, music or cinema, this selection is open to debate and is completely subjective. What is certain is that our 50 greatest goalscorers have provided goals, goals, goals! In total our 50 greatest have scored over 16,500 goals and counting with three of our 50 still actively playing. God Bless the goalkeepers!

In the book I have listed our goalscorers in alphabetical order within each section. It would have been impossible to rank from 50 to 1 or a Top Ten (perhaps the reader may wish to list their own personal choice), all have had distinctive playing careers during very different eras over the course of three separate centuries of league football. Everything has changed: boots, the ball, pitches, formations, hairstyles, the laws and the very interpretations of those laws. Even what players are called, the popularity among Christian names over time. As already stated, the one thing that has remained constant has been the width of the goal and that it does not move.

Goalscorers who did not quite make the starting line-up for our 50 greatest, this time.

Super substitutes list:

Charlie Buchan, 258 top-flight English league goals. Won the league championship with Sunderland in 1912/13 and is also the club record league goalscorer with 209 goals. He created the hugely popular *Buchan's Football Monthly* magazine.

Hughie Ferguson, with 361 league goals, is one of only seven players with 350 or more league goals in English and Scottish league football. A club record 284 of these were with Motherwell. He scored the only goal of the 1927 FA Cup Final for Cardiff City versus Arsenal to take the cup out of England for the first time in history. He returned to Scotland to complete his playing career with Dundee.

Ronnie Allen, 234 league and cup goals in 458 appearances for West Bromwich Albion. Netted twice in the final for WBA to win the FA Cup in 1954 after scoring versus former club Port Vale in the semi-final. First Division top scorer in 1954/55. Autobiography was called *It's Goals That Count*. Would go on to manage his beloved 'Baggies'.

Derek Dougan, 'the Doog', Northern Ireland international, was actually signed for Wolves by Ronnie Allen. He played for Blackburn Rovers versus Wolves in the 1960 FA Cup Final. His partnership with John Richards helped Wanderers reach the 1972 UEFA Cup Final and win the League Cup in 1974. An entertaining Television pundit and one time chairman of the PFA, with over 250 career goals, including 123 with the Wolves.

Martin Chivers, 108 goals for Southampton, spearheading the club's first promotion in season 1965/66 to the top flight. 174 goals for Spurs, scoring in both the winning League Cup Final of 1971 and UEFA Cup Final of 1972. In the 1971/72 season, 'Big Chiv' scored 44 league and cup goals. He also played in Switzerland with Servette.

Francis 'Franny' Lee, "Interesting... very interesting! Just look at his face!" – Barry Davies commentary. Prolific at Bolton Wanderers. Scorer of a record 13 penalties for Manchester City as First Division top scorer with 33 league goals in season 1971/72. He also hit the winner for Man City to win the 1970 European Cup Winners' Cup. Won the league championship with both City and Derby.

Kevin Hector: Top league scorer in 1965/66 with 44 goals for Fourth Division Bradford Park Avenue. League Championship winner twice in the 1970s with Derby County, scoring 201 goals over two spells. In the NASL Kevin won the 1979 Soccer Bowl with the Vancouver Whitecaps.

Les Ferdinand, from non-league football to a goalscoring favourite for top-flight clubs. Goals for QPR helped propel the Hoops to be part of the first season of the Premier League. Lethal with Newcastle United, PFA Player of the Year, scoring 50 goals in just two seasons, twice finishing as league runners up and a League Cup winner with Tottenham in 1999. Over 200 career club goals, 149 Premier League goals.

Supporters' favourite players are usually the ones who lead the line regardless of 'False Nines'. Long live the goalscorer!

Future goalscoring superstars whom one day may be considered for inclusion in any such list of this nature if they maintain and/or improve their present strike rate and avoid injuries and loss of form:

Marcus Rashford, with time on his side. Already his incredible selfless good works through children's meals initiative during the time of coronavirus cannot be praised highly enough. Other young players to keep an eye on are Tammy Abraham, Dominic Calvert-Lewin, and Ivan Toney, Peterborough United and Brentford, who continues to find the net for the Bees in their first top-flight season since 1946/47.

Commentator David Coleman was correct, all those years ago, "Goals pay the rent and Keegan does his share."

I have been fortunate as a matchday going supporter, starting on school trips and as a grown up, to have seen a good few of our greatest goalscorers play live, including 15 of our 50 greatest. It has been a privilege to witness such excellence first hand in the flesh. The art and joy of goalscoring is a beautiful thing that brings so much happiness to all football followers and long may it continue to do so.

Reader's personal choice.
All-time favourite greatest goalscorers.

1. ____________________

2. ____________________

3. ____________________

4. ____________________

5. ____________________

6. ____________________

7. ____________________

8. ____________________

9. ____________________

10. ____________________

Acknowledgements

AFC Bournemouth
arsenalarsenal.net
Aston Villa FC
Airdrieonians FC
Arsenal FC

BBC
Belfast Telegraph
Birmingham Mail
Blackpool FC
BT Sport
Burnley FC
BBC Radio Five Live
Birmingham City FC
Blackburn Rovers FC
Bolton Wanderers FC
Bristol City FC
bullybully.net

Carlisle United FC
Chelsea FC
Crystal Palace FC
Celtic FC
coludata.co.uk

Derby County FC
Daily Mail
Daily Post
Derby Telegraph
Daily Express
Daily Mirror
Daily Record
Daily Telegraph

East Anglian Daily Times
englandstats.com
expressandstar.com
efchertiagesociety.com
Everton FC

FC Barcelona
Fulham FC
FIFA
Four Four Two Magazine

Geoff Hurst Official Website
greensonscreen.co.uk

ianwright8.com
itsroundanditswhite.co.uk
Ipswich Town FC
ITV

lancs.live.co.uk
Leeds United FC
leeds-live.co.uk
Leicester City FC

lfchistory.net
Linfield FC
Liverpool FC
lutontoday.co.uk
Lineker and Baker Podcast
Liverpool Echo
London Evening Standard

malcolmmacdonald.co.uk
Manchester Evening News
Match Football Magazine
Manchester City FC
Manchester United FC
Middlesbrough FC

National Football Museum
Newcastle United FC
norwichcitymyfootballerwriter.com
Newcastle Chronicle
Newport County FC

Oxford United FC

Playfair Football Annuals
premierleague.com
Portsmouth FC

Queen of the South FC
Queens Park Rangers FC

Rangers FC
Robbie Fowler Podcast
RTE
readingfcformerplayers.co.uk
rokerreport.sbnation.com

saintplayers.co.uk
Shoot! Football Magazine
shrimperstrust.co.uk
Sky Sports
southwalesargus.co.uk
stevebloomer.weebly.com
Sunderland AFC
Swansea City FC
Scottish FA
Shrewsbury Town FC
Shropshire Star
Southampton FC
stamford-bridge.com
Stoke City FC
swans100.com

Talksport
The Independent
The Times
The Guardian
The Scotsman
theyflysohigh.co.uk

PRINTED AND BOUND BY:
Copytech (UK) Limited trading as Printondemand-worldwide,
9 Culley Court, Bakewell Road, Orton Southgate.
Peterborough, PE2 6XD, United Kingdom.